Re-Creating Home: Downsizing and De-Cluttering after 50

Fran Scoville
and Holley Ulbrich

ISBN: 1495358313
ISBN 13: 9781495358319
Library of Congress Control Number: 2014901794
CreateSpace Independent Publishing Platform
North Charleston, South Carolina

Table of Contents

Preface

There are lots of books out there to tell you how to simplify your life by reducing the volume of your material possessions and the clutter they create, with tips and suggestions for how to accomplish that goal. While we do offer some ideas about how to de-clutter, it is in the context of something bigger. We are addressing the particular challenges of combining de-cluttering with downsizing in the context of a major life event, which is passing from the householder/ parent/career stage to the grandparent/retiree/mentoring stage. As we re-think the way we live as older adults, the responsibilities we may want to shed and the new ventures we may want to explore, we usually need different surroundings in which those changes can unfold. For many of us who have reached that particular point in life, there is a need to re-evaluate both the home we live in and its contents, acquired during a period of life when we needed that much space and that many things (well, maybe, not quite that many things!).

Hinduism places great emphasis on knowing what we should be doing based on both our role in life and the stage of life we are in. In the Hindu tradition, we have passed through the child/student stage and the householder stage and are ready for the final stage, in which we go inward and remove encumbrances to being a sage, a hermit, a mentor, a wise elder, or whatever it is you see yourself being in the last third of life. Hindus whose hair is white and who have seen their grandsons are directed to dispose of their possessions, go into the forest, and live like a hermit. We may not be ready for quite such a drastic change, but there is insight and wisdom in seeing life to be lived in stages and to make the preparations and adjustments needed for that last stage, preparations that will make those years richer, more meaningful, and more satisfying. Letting go of responsibility for the care and maintenance of a large house and yard full of the accumulations of a lifetime is, for many seniors, an important part of those preparations.

The biggest obstacle to making this adaptation from the second to the third stages of life is not the lack of how-to ideas, although some of them can be quite useful, or even information about your choices and what decisions you need to make. The real challenges are psychological and cultural. The psychological or emotional obstacles include feeling overwhelmed, knowing how to start, keeping yourself motivated, and letting go of your attachment to places and objects and the memories they bear or their monetary value. The cultural obstacles are living in a society that is very focused on consumption and possessions as part of our identities. Once you have come to terms with those obstacles, there is a place for helpful suggestions, and we offer some. But the real focus of this book is accepting and even embracing downsizing as a significant life event for which one must prepare, find support, and learn to think of as a joyful experience.

We want to express thanks to Furman University's Osher Lifelong Learning Institute (OLLI) for their support in writing this book and to members of both the Furman and Clemson University OLLIs for sharing their downsizing experiences in focus groups. We also want to acknowledge our editor, Emily Wood, for her many improvements to the manuscript, and Christine Ulbrich Prado for the original and creative cover design.

Fran Scoville has worked as an extension home economist and a Realtor, moving nine times before retiring back home to South Carolina. From preparing other people's homes to sell to executing her own many moves, Fran has accumulated a wealth of knowledge and experience in downsizing and de-cluttering. She teaches classes in downsizing and de-cluttering for seniors in Clemson and Greenville, South Carolina.

Holley Ulbrich is a retired economics professor from Clemson University in South Carolina and the author of 15 books. She has recently gone through the downsizing experience, moving from her home of 47 years, a 2,500 square foot house with more than an acre of land, to a townhouse in a retirement community with only 60 percent as much space. In retirement, she still teaches two graduate classes a year, teaches short courses for seniors, and is an active community volunteer and a grand-mother of four. Downsizing and de-cluttering has given both Fran and Holley the freedom to enjoy active and satisfying lives in their later years.

PART I

Start With A Vision

One

Downsizing and De-Cluttering

"Less is more." --architect Ludwig Mies van der Rohe

Welcome to the future! The kids are gone—busy accumulating homes, families, and possessions of their own. They have become occasional visitors, hopefully visitors without laundry. All of a sudden you are a family of one or two, rattling around in a house that is bigger than you need or have the energy and desire to maintain. This scenario is the change that prompts many of us to rethink our housing choice.

Sometimes our thoughts about moving or retrofitting our present home are a response to a more specific signal. Retirement is a common trigger for rethinking where we live, now that location is no longer connected to work. Perhaps we are looking for a change of climate, or we would like to live closer to family. Rethinking our physical surroundings can be a response to health problems, to the slowdowns associated with aging bodies, and with that change, a need to shed the physically and mentally demanding tasks of managing a large home and grounds. Sometimes the decision is driven by finances, the need to tap the equity in a home or reduce expenses as income shrinks and/or expenses increase.

Whatever is leading you to think about relocating, your future is likely to call for fewer possessions—less furniture, kitchen equipment, and all the stuff of a lifetime. Downsizing is a housing decision, but if you try to make it happen without de-cluttering, the results will be disastrous. Ideally, de-cluttering is step one, and it can start any time. If you are already considering downsizing, the best time to start the de-cluttering process is right now! It will take some time to make decisions and take action For some of us, de-cluttering may be all we need, perhaps with some adaptation of our present space to our changing needs. But for many of us, this changing situation calls for a different home environment.

In this book, we will walk you through both downsizing and de-cluttering. Chapter 1 is an introduction to housing choices and to grappling with the accumulated possessions of a lifetime. Thinking about houses and contents is just the first step on the road to achieving the life you want. We invite you to explore your thoughts about downsizing and its companion, de-cluttering, as you work through the changes in your life. It is also important to reflect on yourself, because your unique personality, experiences, dreams, and desires will determine what solution works for you (and your partner if you live with someone else). So we start with a preview of downsizing, a little introspection on how you as an individual approach change, and a roadmap through the rest of the book.

The Ups and Downs of Downsizing

Downsizing is something that takes place for most of us as part of a particular stage of life, much like learning to drive in adolescence, discovering your vocation in young adulthood, finding a partner and establishing a home, and all the other events that take place at particular points in a person's life cycle. While downsizing can occur earlier or later, for most of us it takes place between 55 and 80—younger for some, older for others. For some, it never happens at all. Downsizing may mean deciding to share a home with family members or moving closer to where they are. It may mean relocating to a retirement community or letting go of the family home in favor of a townhouse or condo or apartment or assisted living. However you do it, if your home gets smaller, you have to come to terms with your possessions—clothes, books, furniture, decorations, knickknacks, electronics, tools, dishes and kitchen equipment, unfinished projects, materials for hobbies—the list goes on. If you own a home, the house itself is a big part of downsizing, but the big challenge is what to do with the seemingly endless quantity and variety of THINGS.

You will read cheery stories about how liberating downsizing is, how less is more and a smaller home means fewer demands of time and effort and more freedom to do other things, how exciting it is to explore new possibilities about how and where we live. All of these stories are true. You will also hear horror stories of the wrenching pain of parting with cherished possessions and the family home, of the conflict the process creates among family members, of the work it takes to get the house ready to sell and to create a new home, of the heartbreak of leaving the old neighborhood. These stories are also true.

No major change in life is without its sunny side and its shadow, and every person's experience is at least a little bit different. Downsizing alone is both easier and more difficult than downsizing with a partner. Hobbies that require a large yard or a workshop may be lost in the transition. Precious possessions may have difficulty finding loving new owners. Financial considerations may limit your options or force you to make changes you would rather postpone or avoid.

Families who have lived in the same home for a long time are more likely to have trouble letting go and saying goodbye to a place that holds so many memories. Bruce Nemovitz, author of *Moving in the Right Direction,* found in surveys of his senior clientele that 68 percent of them were leaving a home where they had lived for more than 30 years. In order to help you work through the transition, it's important to create a positive vision of the next destination, the next place to call home. That will be our assignment for you at the end of this chapter.

Know Thyself!

There are endless self-help books on the market. They tell you how to lose weight, how to become rich, how to win friends and influence people, and, yes, how to de-clutter and downsize. Some of them will be more helpful than others. One of the keys to downsizing and de-cluttering, or any other kind of self-help project, is to listen thoughtfully to the advice of those who have been there and then figure out how to adapt that advice to your personality, needs, and preferences. De-cluttering books written for 20-somethings may not speak to those over age 50. Introverts approach this challenge differently from extroverts. This book will give you a great deal of advice, but that advice will always be accompanied by the reminder to adapt it to your particular personality and circumstances.

Your authors have explored some of the various personality type schemes in relation to de-cluttering in particular. For this project, we find the Myers-Briggs classification the most helpful. The Myers-Briggs scheme is pretty simple, and it's helpful not only for understanding yourself but for understanding other people and why they respond to the challenge of downsizing and de-cluttering in different ways than you do.

Each of us is defined in the Myers-Briggs system by four pairs of characteristics, one of which is usually more dominant than the other in each person. The first pair of characteristics (E and I) is the most familiar, the extravert (outgoing, energized by interaction with people) and introvert (more reserved, needs more time alone, fatigued by too much interaction). Fran and Holley are both extraverts, married to introverts (a pretty common pattern). The introverts tend to be more reluctant to talk through complicated decisions and may prefer to work alone, which can make the teamwork of downsizing much more difficult.

The second pair of characteristics, the intuitives (N) and the sensors (S), is more complicated to explain, Intuitives tend to be big-picture people, creative types, visionaries. Sensors are more grounded and detail-oriented. Intuitives can visualize the steps that lie ahead to make a transition, but the S will pick up that vision and figure out how to implement it. It's easy to see how these two personality types would approach de-cluttering and downsizing differently, but also how their styles can be complementary. Fran and Holley are both Ns. Fortunately Fran's husband, Phil, is an S, and he helps to fill in the details.

The third pair of characteristics is thinkers (T) and feelers (F). Thinkers approach decluttering and downsizing primarily as a problem to be solved, feelers as an emotional experience. Fs are much more likely to want to keep possessions with sentimental value, while Ts tend to look at objects more from a perspective of usefulness. Holley is a T, as you might expect of an economist, while Fran is an F – more engaged with the energy and the emotions surrounding this life transition. These complementary perspectives, like each of the others, can lead to misunderstanding or a failure to communicate, but they can also be helpful in providing a rounded approach to downsizing and de-cluttering.

Finally, the fourth pair is the judgers (J) and the perceivers (P). Js are the organizers of the world. They make lists and schedules and deadlines and go back to make sure that they carried them out. They tend to be decisive. Ps experience life as a flow and like to gather more information before making a decision. They try to keep their options open. Holley is a J, married to Carl, who is a P, and Fran is a P, married to Phil, who is a J. Again, the difference, whether in a marriage or a writing project, can drive both partners to despair, or it can provide a beautiful balance between rushing to conclusion and wallowing in procrastination.

Each person has a four letter Myers-Briggs "ID." If you string Holley's characteristics together, she is an ENTJ, married to an INFP. Fran is an ENFP, married to her opposite—ISTJ. The "married to" or "partnered with" part is important. You need to know your own personality type in order to figure out what approaches motivate you to undertake and persist in de-cluttering. But you also need to think about the other person or persons who share your space and may approach life very differently.

If you want to learn more about personality types, see the annotated bibliography at the end of this book for some suggestions. There are also other approaches to personality types, including the Enneagram, that may be helpful in reflecting on what makes you think and act the way you do and in guiding you to use your strengths and minimize the effects of your weaknesses in getting your space and your possessions in order for your later years.

By the time you reach the age of 55, your chances for success in any undertaking, solo or shared, are much better if you work with your personality type rather than try to change it! At the same time, de-cluttering and adapting to a downsized living space does require being aware of your habits and which ones need to change. It is generally believed that it takes at least three weeks to develop a new good habit or break an old one—more for some habits than others. It is probably easier to train yourself to hang the keys on a key rack than to quit smoking. So as we emerge from the de-cluttering process into maintenance in the final chapter, it is important to convert some of the changes that you have made in your daily rounds into habits that make life easier and more enjoyable.

Because we respect individual differences, we don't offer a one-size-fits-all plan for downsizing and de-cluttering. Instead, we offer stories, shared experiences, and the wisdom of others as a menu from which you can select the approach that works for you. At the end of each chapter, there will be an assignment that invites you to take some of the material in this chapter and figure out how it works for you as you embark on the adventure of downsizing and de-cluttering.

Five Stages Toward your New Life

Downsizing and de-cluttering involves five distinct stages: committing, de-cluttering, choosing, transitioning, and settling in. The first and often most difficult stage is committing. You have to decide that you are ready to make a change of some kind in the reasonably near future, and then you need to prepare to explore your options—on your own, with your partner, with your family, or with the advice and support of your friends. Chapters 2 and 3 explore the obstacles and rewards as you decide whether or not to commit to a process of changing your space in a significant and lasting way.

The second and third stages are the action steps of de-cluttering and choosing. These two stages can proceed simultaneously, because de-cluttering is essential to any housing choice you may make. Chapters 4 thorough 6 help you to manage the de-cluttering process, disposing of possessions in ways that are satisfying and meaningful and that honor the memories, sentiment, and value of what you sell or give to others.

Choosing means identifying all the options and weighing the pros and cons of each choice—whether to move, where to live, and what kind of home to choose. Chapters 7 and 8 help you explore your options and find resources to help you implement your choice.

The fourth stage is transition. Here we address the practical issues of preparing your home for sale while simultaneously acquiring another one. Unless you are moving to an apartment, you will probably be dealing with real estate and banking professionals at this point. Chapter 9 will provide some general guidance on what kinds of decision you need to make and where to look for professional help in what is often a complicated and confusing process.

Stage five is the fun part—settling down in your new home and discovering a different lifestyle with new neighbors and new possibilities. If you were attentive to the de-cluttering process, you want to keep the accumulation of possessions from taking over your new life. So in Chapter 10 we offer some guidance in maintenance so that you can enjoy your new home and surroundings as much as you once enjoyed the home of your working and child-raising years.

Five Stages of Downsizing and De-Cluttering

Step One: Committing
Step Two: De-Cluttering
Step Three: Choosing
Step Four: Transition
Step Five: Settling In

All five of these stages are about making and implementing decisions—decisions about staying put or relocating, decisions about dealing with clutter, decisions about where you will move and what kind of home you want to have. Decisions are hard work, whether you are making them alone or with a partner. Every decision forecloses some options that we might have preferred. Every decision requires weighing and gathering information, listening to our head, our heart, and our gut for what seems right and feels right, and then taking action. Often the action is easier than the deciding! The emphasis in this book is on guiding you through a decision process that works for you—your particular situation, needs, preferences, and way of being in the world.

So let's get started!

Assignment: Creating a Vision

Each chapter is this book has a homework assignment. We recommend that you get yourself a notebook and write down the questions and your answers for each assignment for future reference. Even if you don't refer back to what you wrote, the exercise of writing it out will help clarify your thinking.

For this chapter, the assignment is visioning. Think about the life you want to be living in the future. You decide how far ahead into the future you want to plan—five years, ten years, twenty years?

What do you want life to be like in five, ten, or twenty years? Where will you be living—in your present home, in another home in the same area, or in a different place altogether? We will explore these choices in more detail later, but it's a good idea to start thinking about staying in the same area or moving elsewhere right now. So pick a time frame—ten years is good—and imagine the areas were you would like to be living—United States or elsewhere, same state or different, north or south, east or west, coast or mountains, urban or rural or in between.

A second important question is, what will occupy your time, your energy, and your attention? Is it travel, hobbies, outdoor recreation, grandchildren, volunteer work, gardening, writing? If you live with a partner, both of you need to do this exercise and share your visions with each other. How will the activities you and your partner envision affect your choice of where to live?

Third question: What health challenges might you need to take into account? Do you have developing problems with vision, hearing, mobility, or a family history of those problems? Does your partner? Is one (or both) of you likely to need some kind of support in terms of medical care, transportation, meals, or daily activities? Health challenges should figure into what kind of home you choose, but proximity to support services and to family may also affect the area in which you choose to live.

The final step for this first assignment is to give some thought to what kind of home would fit into that vision. We will get to the details later, but for now just a general sketch will do. Is that place your present home, de-cluttered and retrofitted with grab bars and wider doorways? Or is it a different place, perhaps smaller and with fewer maintenance demands? Is it in your present community or far away? Do you want to have a yard where you can garden? Is this home close to shopping and recreation or out in the country, near the water or the mountains, close to family or close to the friends and neighbors you have acquired where you are? This home will be the place where you carry out your vision. The right home makes it more likely that you will be able to do just that.

PART II

Committing To Change

Two

Engaging the Spirit

You are not your stuff.—Fran Scoville

I f you have been in your home for a while, any effort to think about downsizing and/or relocating is likely to encounter a lot of inertia. Change of any kind is threatening, a source of anxiety, and this particular kind of change is even more challenging because it lends itself to procrastination. It's not like having our first baby, where we have a nine-month time frame in which to figure out how to adapt and, once set in motion, no ability to put if off. With downsizing and de-cluttering, we don't have a clear deadline, and, in consequence, some of us wait until it is too late. In addition, we may feel that we don't have the energy or the physical ability to cope with moving, discarding, rethinking, and adapting. We may tell ourselves it is easier to stick with the familiar than risk the unknown and make the effort to bring about the changes we know we should make.

This chapter is about the emotional and spiritual dimension of coping with a big change in your life. We will identify some of the obstacles, the fears, the anxieties, the sources of resistance that you are likely to encounter as you set out on this journey. There is going to be some letting go. Letting go of attachment to our place of comfort, safety, and memory, and letting go of possessions that help to define who we are and also carry memories, are necessary but difficult undertakings. As Catholic priest and best-selling author Richard Rohr says in *Falling Upward: Spirituality for the Second Half of Life,* we spend the first part of our lives building a container—an identity, a family, a career, a home. The rewarding challenge for the second half of life is to let the container go. He also says that the journey of the soul is one of always leaving home—that place of safety where we have become secure and comfortable and rooted.

Most of the homes we leave are not physical dwellings. They may be college, job, groups of friends we have outgrown, organizations we to which we no longer wish to belong. But right now we are focusing on the house as a physical structure rather than the home as a state of being. We also are concentrating on the obstacles you will encounter and the opportunities you make a new house into a home in this new stage of life.

Overcoming Fear and Anxiety

Inside every 55 year old person is that invincible adolescent who sees life as an adventure, paddling along in a canoe, wondering only casually what is around the next bend in the river and hoping only half-heartedly that it isn't a waterfall. Somewhere between the ages of 18 and 30 most of us reach the "...and they lived happily ever after" part of the fairy tale and engage ourselves in the daily-ness of living. But when it comes to downsizing and de-cluttering, that inner adolescent is exactly the person we need to engage. We need to rally the part of ourselves that is ready to set out on the next adventure, the adventure that comes after the education, the career, the home-buying, the child-raising. Suddenly we see the children set out on their own, we see retirement looming, and what do we do?

We often lose that sense of life as a journey, in which each stage has its own frustrations and its own joys. We also get accustomed to gradual change as we age, move on in our careers, watch our children grow up, and we fail to notice the cumulative effect of those changes. Our hair may be turning gray, our knees may not hold up as well as they once did, we may realize that we are never going to climb Mount Everest, and we start getting senior discounts at restaurants and movie theaters. But in our heads, we are forever 40—or 30. And despite wobbly knees and gray hair, there is still the possibility of adventure ahead of us.

Whatever precipitates change—the accumulation of slow, gradual changes or more dramatic events such as empty nest, loss of a life partner, or retirement—we need to recognize the event and that it confronts us with the need to change in response. These changes offer both an opportunity and a challenge to rediscover our inner adolescent and seek to joyfully embrace those changes that frustrate, frighten, and enrich us.

The biggest obstacle to change is fear and anxiety. In response to surveys of people between 72 and 83 who were downsizing, Bruce Nemovitz found that some of the major fears expressed were moving to unfamiliar surroundings; the challenge of packing, sorting, and disposing of stuff; financial concerns; and possible loss of control or independence. Another source of fear and anxiety was getting a home ready to sell and going through the selling process. Downsizing (or not) is a very big life decision, and the fear of making a costly mistake can hold people back.

How do we overcome fear? If a fear is based on uncertainty or lack of information, that's a matter of reason. It is a signal to gather information so we can make informed decisions (see next section). But if a fear is about change, about loss, about risk, then it is grounded in emotion. Then it is time to call on your personal support system to talk through your fears. It is also a good idea to consult individuals who have been through the downsizing and de-cluttering process, especially individuals who have experienced the kind of downsized situation you find most appealing. One of your authors did just that: looking at townhouses in a nearby retirement community, she consulted with friends who lived there about the pros and cons, the costs and constraints, the balance of neighborliness and privacy, whether her pets would be in a good situation. Those conversations helped to address a lot of her concerns, even if she couldn't anticipate them all.

When fears see the light of day, particularly in conversation with someone who has worked through similar concerns, those fears tend to shrink to a manageable size, much like the monsters under the bed that turn out to be dust bunnies or dirty socks in the morning. But sometimes fears surrounding a particular option are justified. If they are, it is better to know before committing, so that you can explore other options, including the option of staying put.

Obstacles: Why not Procrastinate?

Overcoming procrastination requires an effort of the will, and will has to be cultivated through actions, starting small and building momentum. The lack of a clear deadline is itself a major obstacle to change of all kinds, whether it is downsizing, breaking a bad habit, cleaning the house, or almost anything else in life. When we were younger, living with parents and going to school, deadlines were set for us. As adults, we have deadlines at work, but much of the rest of life leaves us free to make our own timetables.

In the Myers-Briggs personality type system, it is the Js and Ps who respond to this challenge very differently. The J (judging) personality type makes lists, creates order, sets priorities, makes deadlines, and needs closure. The P (perceiving) personality type experiences life more as a flow and is usually tempted to gather more information before committing. (Those of us who are Js think the P stands for procrastinating! And the Ps may think it stands for Puzzled by the often frenetic and hyper-organized operating style of many Js.) If you are a J, your challenge is more likely to be learning to avoid rushing to judgment, but also enlisting the co-operation of any P's in your life who may see beyond the urgency of taking action. If you are not a J, you may need to find one to work with you, perhaps a friend or a professional organizer or a real estate professional.

Many years ago, a letter to Dear Abby asked about whether the writer should consider going to college. The woman was 36 years old and was concerned that, by college graduation, she would be 40. Abby's answer? How old will you be in four years if you don't go to college? Twenty years later, the opposite problem exists for many of us. I'm only 60, or 65, and I'm still doing okay in my present situation, so why should I bother to change or plan for change? The answer is, if you wait too long, it may be too late to make such a big life change, because of the demands it places on us physically, mentally, and emotionally. So the time to prepare is always now, even if the preparations consist only of baby steps like selecting a part of your house to de-clutter, talking to your children about possessions and the family home, and/or gathering information about places you might like to live.

Obstacles: Resistance to Organizing and De-Cluttering

The emotional obstacles to de-cluttering and creating an organized space are somewhat different from those that keep us from downsizing or relocating in response to a different stage of life. The classic book on home organization was Stephanie Winston's *Getting Organized,* published in 1978. She sees the emotional issue as an unresolved tension from childhood and adolescence called compliance/defiance. How many times did most of us hear, "clean up your room! Pick up your mess!" Part of us wanted to cooperate with Mom (it was almost always Mom), but part of us wanted to assert our independence by doing it our own way, or not at all. We carry those inner battles into adulthood. There are still people who are battling with that interior tape of a parental authority figure into their 60s and 70s, long after the parent has died or lost interest in how tidy their child's home is. Winston believes that we are all born with an inherent capacity and desire for order and organization, but they often fall victim to the adolescent drive for creating an independent identity.

Cheer up! If you have a messy house and adolescent children, perhaps they will rebel by creating order in their own lives or helping you create more order in yours. In any case, it's time to call a truce with your adolescent self and move on with your life. If you didn't have a yearning for more order and organization and less chaos, you wouldn't be reading this book.

Obstacles: It's Overwhelming!

Fran has had a lot of experience helping people get started in the de-cluttering process, which is essential to downsizing whether you are moving or staying put. Breaking the task into smaller parts is important. Fran is a big believer in techniques that enable us to focus. Buddhists talk about our "monkey mind"—that constant inner chatter as well as the external distractions that keep us from getting anything done. So focusing is very important. Perhaps you need to find a time when you have the house to yourself, turn off the television, sit for five minutes with your eyes closed, and get centered. Or you may have another technique that works for you. It's important to start the process when you expect to have some uninterrupted time, even if you don't use it all. Fran notes that sometimes the problem with inability to focus is actually a literal focusing problem, located in the eyes rather than the emotions. So if the inability to focus has been part of your life in general, not just de-cluttering, you may want to have your vision checked by an optometrist!

Fran also recommends that you start each day by focusing on the five A's: awaken (to your surroundings), awareness (of what needs to be done), assess (deciding what to tackle), action, and appreciation (patting yourself on the back for a job well done). Several professional organizers recommend the value of simple rituals in jump-starting your efforts. Get dressed, even if you aren't going to leave home. Make the bed—it makes the whole room look orderly. These simple steps are energizing. Clutter drains energy, and order restores it.

Clutter didn't happen overnight, so give yourself some time. Start by taking on a small but manageable task, such as cleaning out a kitchen drawer or a cupboard. Set a timer—you can get one at the drug store or use the one on your microwave—for fifteen minutes. If you finish before the timer goes off, you can pat yourself on the back or go on to another drawer or cupboard. If the timer goes off before you are done, you can leave it till later or reset the timer. That's Fran's favorite technique. For Holley, the favorite method is ten things rather than 15 minutes. Finding ten things to recycle in some fashion—to give away, donate, sell, or put in the recycling bin—is a regular weekly event in her household. Books, clothes, and kitchen equipment are the usual suspects. Picking up and putting away ten things to make a room tidier is another easy way to create order.

Yet another way to get over the hump of getting started is to pick a place or a group of objects to focus on until it is done. For Holley, it was the 5,000+ slides occupying 36 slide carousels that were taking up most of a closet. For others, it may be a place—a workshop, a home office, a coat closet, an attic. Don't think ahead to the next challenge; just focus your attention on this one, 15 minutes, 15 objects, or one carousel of slides at a time.

Obstacles: Hoarding, Collecting, and Sentiment

Why are some things so difficult to let go of? Many of us have seen hoarders on TV reality shows, and we probably know some hoarders among our friends, family, and neighbors. Their homes are so full of stuff that they can barely move, sometimes creating a health hazard. Most of us are not hoarders in the pathological sense, but we are all probably attached to some possessions, items we think we just can't part with. Two types of possessions in particular are difficult to let go. One is collections. Some people collect dolls, others firearms, postage stamps, stuffed animals, autographs, books, and even (in the case of Holley's daughter), bottle caps. Some collections don't take up much space, while others are voluminous or require shelves, walls, or even entire rooms for their display. So take a moment and count your collections. How many collections do you have? Most women have at least one clothing-related collection: shoes, or purses, or scarves. For Fran, the challenging collection was soup tureens. For Holley, it was books, shelves and shelves of them.

Letting go of or paring down collections can be especially difficult. If the collection has value, the satisfaction of selling it to someone who will value it as much as you do may help break the logjam of "de-collecting." A family member or a museum may want your collection intact, and you can part with it knowing it will either stay in the family or be displayed publicly for all to enjoy.

Another type of possession that is difficult to let go of is the one with sentimental value, and most homes are full of such well-loved memorabilia. It's not the object itself but the memories that are attached to it that we don't want to let go. That's why people buy souvenirs on vacations, because the souvenirs remind them of the experience. Other items were gifts that remind us of the giver. We need to remind ourselves that we don't have to get rid of everything, we just need to pare it down. In later chapters we will address some of the ways of letting go that provide satisfaction, as well as some ways to choose what to keep and what to let go.

In our focus groups, we heard a number of creative suggestions for dealing with sentimental items. One woman had several family quilts that were deteriorating, but the fabrics held memories of dresses or occasions. She cut out the best and most significant pieces, framed them with notes on the back, and shared them with her children and grandchildren. Several took pictures, which take up much less space than piles of stuffed animals, knickknacks, dishes, and other forms of lovely clutter—but still clutter. Most often, our focus group participants chose to let one or just a few items from the collection carry the memories for all of them, and they dispersed the rest to charity, museums, family members, or yard sales.

Obstacles: The Spirit is Willing but the Partner is Not

If you share your home with someone else—a spouse or partner, a child or parent, for example—you may have additional obstacles to downsizing and decluttering. Are you going to share a new space or continue together in the present space? Are there family members who no longer live with you but are attached to your home the way it is and was and therefore, in their minds, always should be? If this change is going to involve other people, engaging their co-operation may be a challenge. You may be living with a hoarder, a collector, or just someone who doesn't pay attention to the volume of stuff that has accumulated over the years. That person may be reluctant to participate in downsizing and de-cluttering for some of the same reasons as you have been reluctant to get started. Or your children may be resistant to change. They may have their stuff stored at your house and be unwilling to claim it, or they may want to be in that home for holidays and bring your grandchildren to visit you there. For them, the house is a museum of memories. For you, it is a place in which you live your life, and who wants to live in a museum?

If you have been married a long time, chances are you have developed a style of resolving conflicts. You will need to draw on that experience now, and perhaps refine and polish it or even get intervention from a third party. All the skills you developed in deciding how to raise the children, where to go on vacation, how to manage the family finances, and what to have for dinner will be called into play for this major life change. Those skills reflect ways of resolving conflicts that arise from differences in personality, upbringing, interests, and energy.

Julie Morgenstern's *Organizing from the Inside Out* has an excellent chapter on dealing with the partnership aspect of de-cluttering, whether that partner is spouse, parent, child, or roommate. It's important to treat that person with respect, to protect some of his/her possessions, and to work on the challenge of accepting the things the other person absolutely wants to keep.

When Frank and Rita moved from a three story house in Pennsylvania to the beach condo in South Carolina they had owned for ten years, Frank wanted to bring all the furniture. Rita had to convince him it was impossible (they already had furniture!) by measuring the rooms and the furniture, making cutouts of the furniture, and challenging him to arrange it. That did the trick.

There are a few other techniques that might help jump-start the de-cluttering process when you are approaching it with others. One is to enlist outside help. Family members, friends, or paid assistance are all possibilities. Sometimes a life partner is not the best person to work with on such a project, just as parents are often not the best people to teach their children to drive. All the other tensions in the relationship can come to bear on this particular activity. Better to spend that time with your partner or child or parent on mutual enjoyment than on challenging tasks.

Holley's husband, Carl, was a master of cluttering, particularly in his home office and in the basement, where he had his tools, his sailing supplies, and his framing shop. Once a year Holley paid her son-in-law to work with Carl in cleaning and organizing the shop, and occasionally she enlisted her youngest daughter to work with her Dad in organizing his cluttered office. When it came to downsizing, there were two trained staffers to help with the work!

A second technique is to start with yourself. Clean out your books, your home office, your closet and dresser, your kitchen if you are the main cook and bottle washer. Then invite your partner to appreciate how much more pleasant this organized space is, and invite him or her to do the same in his space, with whatever help he or she needs and finds acceptable.

A third and last-resort technique is to de-clutter while the other person is away. This method is the easiest, but be aware that it is fraught with danger. If you are going to try this approach, be sure to set aside a pile of questionable items to go through before your housemate returns.

Just remember that you and the person or persons with whom you share your home probably have many of the same obstacles when it comes to de-cluttering. Talk through some of them and set a goal or timetable for making decisions, de-cluttering, and settling in a new or renovated space. A positive vision of what life will be like at the other end of the tunnel can be a powerful motivator for everyone involved.

Opportunities: Voluntary Simplicity

Voluntary simplicity means making the choice to live more simply. It doesn't necessarily mean becoming a hermit in the woods or embracing poverty. Both a movement and an individual choice, it has an ancient history among the monastics of many religious traditions. It also has a long history in some of the religious communities that arose from the radical wing of the Protestant Reformation like the Amish and the Mennonites, as well as the communes of the 19th century (like the Shakers) and more recently in the non-religious ("hippie") communes that sprung up in the 1960s in the United States.

Today's version of voluntary simplicity is an intentional, non-mainstream lifestyle that emphasizes the basics, the things that matter. It reminds us to think about what we accumulate and what we need in the way of possessions and services. This can mean consciously choosing a smaller home, less furniture, fewer electronic gadgets, using alternative transportation, and/or more creation of our own consumption through gardening, cooking, sewing and home repairs. Voluntary simplicity may involve a compost heap, a human-powered lawn mower, or solar panels on your roof.

Voluntary simplicity doesn't necessarily mean a less satisfying lifestyle. It should be more satisfying because you are more aware of yourself, your priorities, and your needs, more engaged in creating and sustaining your own life support system instead of outsourcing it to others. Voluntary simplicity enables us to give less time and attention to the acquisition and maintenance of material possessions in order to redirect our time, energy, and resources to other priorities.

Voluntary simplicity is much broader than our specific focus on the physical objects that occupy our space, time, and attention. Downsizing has some kinship with voluntary simplicity, but it is different in that it is a response to a particular stage in life rather than a long term lifestyle. In downsizing, some voluntary simplicity is appropriate, but it is important to avoid being overly critical of either our own past or the choices made by others about acquiring and enjoying stuff. The stuff has served its purpose, and it is time to let it go. You may embark on downsizing and find yourself embracing voluntary simplicity, or you may stop well short of such a dramatic change and simply rethink what you need and want (and what you don't) in terms of your home and your possessions. Voluntary simplicity is introduced merely as additional tool that may be helpful in thinking about your journey through downsizing and de-cluttering.

Opportunities: Less is More

In our focus groups, we heard over and over again that getting rid of possessions, whether staying in place or relocating, is very liberating. Fewer things and less clutter make it easier to find things. Having 100 CDs instead of 600 not only frees up space but also makes you aware of what you have. Just like a leaner closet highlights the clothing you like and wear, rather than surrounding them with the clutter of the ones you don't wear. Less furniture makes the room more attractive, more flexible, and more navigable. Getting rid of the generational heritage of china and glassware means that your cupboards are more adequate and it is easier to find things in your kitchen. Most people in our focus groups reported that, after the difficulty of getting started, de-cluttering was very rewarding, very satisfying, and very freeing.

Remember Carl, who was a clutterer and a pack rat? Carl never discarded anything. When he couldn't find something, he went out and bought another one. When he moved to a nursing home, Holley and her helper discovered that he owned 12 hammers. In his desk were 28 containers of dental floss and fifteen nail clippers. Not only is it costly and wasteful to have so many duplicates, it is also harder to find them or anything else in all the clutter!

Opportunities: the Joy of Giving

Giving things away can be one of the most rewarding parts of downsizing and de-cluttering. Finding a good home with just the right person for a treasure you no longer need ensures that it will continue to be valued.

Both Fran and Holley have stories to share about their husbands' collections of National Geographic magazines. People who subscribe to this magazine frequently save them—in Carl's case, in slip cases—even if they never go back and reread them. Both Carl and Phil had large collections going back several decades and were reluctant to let them go, but they eventually agreed. Then began the process of finding someone who wanted them. Holley's experience was the easiest. Advertising on Freecycle, she was contacted by several home schooling parents who saw them as a valuable resource in their children's education.

Phil had tried libraries and other outlets with no luck, so Fran persuaded him to put them on the curb for recycling pickup. Over the course of the day, the pile began to shrink, until it was entirely gone, although neither Fran nor Phil saw who was taking them. That evening, their neighbor called and asked if it was all right that her ten-year-old son had taken possession of the magazines. He liked them better than video games! The son met with Phil to thank him for the gift, and Phil felt much happier about letting go.

Linda (a focus group participant) had some family pictures from pre-war Poland. In a class on de-cluttering, she spoke of the need to find a home for them. No family members were interested. A museum turned out to be the best suggestion, and today her pictures are part of a display in a Texas museum with other pictures from the same era, some of them other distant relatives!

Some adult children experience a feeling of abandonment when their parents sell the family home and move to smaller quarters—even if they haven't really lived there since they went off to college. Give them a chance to say goodbye. They may want cuttings of plants, pictures of home, or certain objects like paintings that will help them say goodbye. But it is, after all, your home and your life. In most cases, your children have homes of their own now, and it may be necessary to remind them (and yourselves) that they aren't entitled to yours as well.

What do you want to leave to your children or other heirs? Probably, you want to leave them good memories and some family heirlooms, perhaps other objects that are useful or valuable or carry happy memories. Giving within the family, and realizing that your children or other family members value both the possessions and the memories they carry, is a source of joy. But they need to be the ones to decide what they want. You can offer, but they need to be free to take what they want and leave you to dispose of the rest. Children typically do not relish the prospect of cleaning out their parents' home in the future. If you present your downsizing and de-cluttering project in a positive light, they will most likely be relieved, perhaps even relieved enough to pitch in with the process now. Having an impossible mess to clean up is probably not what you or they had in mind as an inheritance. Chapter 5 offers some suggestions on ways to give your prized possessions to those who will cherish them most.

More difficult for some people is the absence of direct heirs, or the reality of children who are distant and uninterested. What will happen to my possessions when I am gone? Later chapters will offer some ideas. Whether your heirs are family members, friends, or a charitable organization, culling what you have is an important first step for whoever inherits your possessions.

Opportunities: New Experiences

Many of the people in our downsizing focus groups reported that they were pleasantly surprised at how freeing themselves from the past—the big house and yard, the possessions, the financial obligations—empowered them to try new things, make new friends, explore new places, and not only check off items on their "bucket lists" but add new ones as they went along. Whether it was travel, new hobbies, learning experiences, or more intentional time for family and friends, the ways in which they spent their days and weeks was more satisfying, more rewarding, and less stressful. The tunnel from here to there may look long and dark, but there is light at the end of the tunnel, and it's not a freight train headed in your direction.

It's the light of a new day, with all the hope and promise any new day carries with it.

> ## Assignment: Engaging your Emotional Support System
>
> Several times in this chapter we have encouraged you to reach out to others to help you clear away some of the cobwebs, address the emotions, and answer the questions you have about a very big decision. One group you can turn to is family and friends, beginning with your spouse and/ or grown children if you have them. Remember, spouses can help or hinder the downsizing and de-cluttering process, and the style of interaction you have developed over your years of marriage will be tested as you attempt to work through both the decision and the process of downsizing. Friends who have been through the experience can be invaluable sources of information, advice and encouragement, even though you will have to adapt their input to your own needs, preferences, and personality type.
>
> From Alcoholics Anonymous and Weight Watchers to families of patients with life-threatening illnesses, we can learn an important lesson from the rise of support groups: life's difficult experiences are made easier by knowing that you are not alone. Others all around us are going through the same struggles. Since downsizing and de-cluttering are both rewarding experiences as well as difficult ones, it's important to celebrate with others. Tell your support system about your big victories, like deciding to sell your home and buy a condominium, but also remember to tell them about the small ones, like cleaning out the closet full of photos.
>
> There are also other resources that can be helpful, such as life coaches, Senior Relocation Specialists, and

professional organizers. There are even on-line de-cluttering support groups where you can share your concerns and your experiences. Your assignment is to identify the key players in your emotional support system and reflect on how they might support or assist you in this undertaking. Make a list of people that offer emotional support. Make a date with them, one at a time or in a group, and talk through your feelings about making a change in your life. Ask for their encouragement, support, and assistance, and offer to do the same for them if they are going through the same process. Make plans to see them regularly (or stay in contact through social media) and keep them up to date on your progress, including any obstacles you encounter and how you address them.

Three

Getting Started:

Engaging the Mind

"Begin with the end in mind." --Steven Covey

W e started addressing obstacles and opportunities associated with downsizing by considering the spirit or emotions,
because that's where much of the resistance to change is located.
But there are also obstacles (and opportunities) in the reasoning,
calculating part of our being that we need to name, claim, and
address. This chapter focuses on the primary obstacles in the
logical, analytical part of our being: concerns about money, in-
complete information, and/or a lack of clear and ordered goals.
We also explore the positive outcomes: the opportunity to create a home that meets your present and expected future needs
and a chance to let go of some of your responsibilities.

Don't expect everything to happen overnight. Fran estimates that, once the commitment has been made, the actual
process of transition from information gathering to settling in
typically takes from one to two years.

*Bart and Elaine were in their late seventies and had lived
in their home for fifty years—Bart for the first 10 years with*

his first wife, with his second wife, Elaine, and her daughter joining him and his three children for the next 40. They had always been very attentive to the details of daily living, handling spending, time, health care, recreation, travel, food, and other aspects of household management with care and intentionality. But now they were in denial about their declining vision, mobility, and general health. They were also somewhat overwhelmed by the task of dealing with the 50-year accumulation of possessions that needed to be sorted and moved or discarded or repurposed.

Eventually they came to terms with the fact that they were at a stage in life where they needed to be closer to friends and transportation, as well as in a house more suited to their increasing physical limitations. Once they overcame the obstacles of procrastination, denial, and lack of direction, they tackled the task of relocating to more suitable housing with the same methodical attention to detail that they had given to the rest of their life together. For Bart and Elaine, money was not a major issue: an adequate income meshed nicely with lifelong habits of frugality. Nor was location a question; they agreed that they wanted to remain in the immediate area with many friends close by. But they knew that they had a lot of decisions to make in terms of where to live, what kind of home to buy, and how best to deal with a lifetime of possessions from a blended family.

Bart and Elaine began the process by talking to friends. They were fortunate to have several close friends who had made the same transition and could share their experiences in relocating within that same community. Fifty years in the same place had built up a network of contacts, information sources, and knowledge of options on which they could draw. It took them several years to come to terms with the need to relocate, but, once they overcame the emotional challenges, they were ready to face the problem-solving part of the task, and that moved much faster.

Obstacles: Money

So where do we start? If we are being analytical, money is a good starting point. It's not true that most retirees live on a fixed income as they once did. Social Security is adjusted for inflation, and so are some pensions. Investments wisely managed usually yield returns that are higher than the rate of inflation. In addition, many people over 65 are still working. In 1980, only 3.3 percent of the labor force was made up of people over age 65. By 2010, that figure had risen to 5.4 percent, which amounted to 6.7 million people. But many older people, retired or still working, feel uncertainty about their financial future. How long they can continue to work? What will happen to medical care? Housing costs? Will they outlive their assets? Making a housing change can increase that uncertainty, but it can also decrease it.

Each of the housing options explored in the Chapters 7 and 8 has a financial dimension. Some moves will cost more money, some less. Some require upfront cash—preparing your house for sale and closing costs on a new home, for example—but will save money in the long run. A smaller home will mean less spent on maintenance and lower utility bills and property taxes, but it may involve fees to a homeowners' association.

Many older people are hesitant to consider downsizing because they are unaware of some of the financial options available to help them bridge from old home to new home. We will look at some of the financing options in Chapter 9. But each person's financial situation is unique, so you probably want to talk to a trusted financial advisor as well as a mortgage banker to have a clearer picture of how to handle the financial dimension of downsizing.

Obstacles: Clarifying Goals

Bruce Nemovitz surveyed people who were downsizing (ages ranged from 72 and 83) and found that the number one reason to downsize was maintenance—the responsibilities of maintaining a home or yard. 42 percent of his respondents listed that as one of their three main reasons for downsizing. Second was health issues with 34 percent Other reasons included the present home being too large, loneliness, transportation, and finances.- Similarly, a poll by AP-NORC Center for Public Affairs Research showed that most Americans over 40 say that they want a one level home with no stairs that is close to their children and medical care. These concerns and this vision offer a starting point for picturing the kind of home you would like to have.

Clarifying goals requires some intentional listening to yourself, and your partner if you have one. Here is an exercise that might help. The list on the following page notes some possible goals for your next 20 years of life. The first step is to add to the list any personal goals that are missing. Then review your expanded list. You may need to set some priorities, because you may not be able to accomplish all of these goals.

One technique for ranking is to give yourself 100 points to spend and allocate them among the various. Perhaps better storage space is worth 15 points, handicapped accessibility 10, less house/yard maintenance 10, the opportunity to garden 15. If you use up your 100 points before everything that matters gets points, you will have to rework you point distribution. This prioritized list will help you think about which goals are important and how you can work toward accomplishing them.

A second way to set goals is to identify family members or friends who have made a life change at this stage and seem to be satisfied with their new situations. Talk to them about the changes they made and how those changes made life easier, better, or more satisfying. This kind of conversation may give you some insight into what you want to see change in your own life.

Finally, one goal that is not on the list is peace of mind. All of us know that change is ahead of us as we reach our 50s and 60s. Confronting that change directly and altering our living situation in anticipation of that change will make the experience as positive as possible. It is a good way to overcome fear, uncertainty, and frustration.

General goals

- Support group of family and/or friends
- More discretionary income
- Climate
- Access to water or mountains

House goals

- Handicapped accessibility (grab bars, wide doorways, no stairs)
- Less house/yard maintenance
- Less clutter and "stuff" to deal with
- Opportunity to garden
- Better storage space

Activity goals

- Travel
- Part time work

•Volunteer in the community
•Fitness/exercise
•Outdoor recreation
•Intellectual/cultural stimulation
•Hobbies and/or crafts

Obstacles: Information

We live in an information society. If anything, we suffer from too much information. Information can be clutter too! But when we are trying to make decisions, we do need information, and we need to know where to find it. Below are some of the specific kinds of information you will need as you make plans to downsize:

- How to de-clutter your present home, whether you decide to move or not
- How to adapt your present home to your changing needs, and what it will cost
- What housing options are available in your present community or the community to which you would like to relocate, and their cost
- The advantages and disadvantages of the various kinds of housing (single family detached, townhouse, condominium, apartment) and various types of communities (gated community, condominium complex, subdivision, new urban development, retirement community, etc.)
- Your financing options
- What education, recreation, and entertainment options are available in the new area

We will explore these topics in the next six chapters. Hopefully, this list will help you know some of the important questions to ask before you start looking for answers. For specific kinds of information and options, the internet is a good place to start. For local information, try family, friends, and neighbors. Start talking to people, especially those who have already made some kind of transition We will point you to some resources in the rest of this book, including the annotated bibliography at the end, but, in the meantime, it is a good idea to start making a list of questions as they come to you.

Opportunities: Making a Home for Who You Are Now

As we noted in Chapter 1, if you are reading this book, you have likely reached a stage of life—fewer people living in your home, retirement, or perhaps health and/or financial issues—that is propelling you to make a change in your housing situation. The above goals assessment should provide you with a clearer perspective on any gap between where you are living now and where you would like to be living. This gap represents an opportunity to make your life better. Perhaps downsizing will make life easier because it frees up financial resources as you reclaim the equity in your home. It may give you a financial cushion after buying a new home and also lower monthly expenses. Your new, smaller home may be easier to maintain, or it may be better adapted to emerging health considerations with wider doorways, grab bars in the bathroom, and no stairs to climb. It may be closer to family and friends, or opportunities to engage in lifelong learning, volunteer, or enjoy more cultural events and recreation. Looked at from this perspective, downsizing is more about trading than giving things up.

The size of the home and the kind of home you choose will determine your expenses and your responsibilities. It may limit some of your opportunities to pursue hobbies or other interests, or it may enhance those pursuits. A small home that is well laid out may be more easily adapted than your present home to creating a wood shop, a gardening area, a sewing room, a scrapbooking space, or other kinds of hobbies.

Location is the key to putting yourself in the position to take advantage of opportunities to strengthen relationships and pursue leisure activities. Whether you choose a retirement community, a smaller detached home, a condo, or even an apartment, and whether you stay close to where you are or move some distance away, your choice of a community is as important as the kind of home you choose within that community.

Opportunities: Letting Go of Responsibilities

For many of us, an important goal when downsizing is reduced responsibilities. A newer and smaller home typically requires less interior maintenance and often has features that make it easier to maintain than an older home. A smaller yard, or no yard responsibilities, is another major form of letting go—usually with relief! If you enjoy gardening, you likely will not object to giving up mowing the grass in exchange for more time and energy to give to your garden.

If you decide to move to a gated community or a retirement community or a condominium, many of the maintenance responsibilities will now fall to the homeowner's association (HOA). While you will pay for services in the form of HOA fees, you may find it less expensive to buy those services "in bulk" through a homeowner's association, especially if you are already paying for help with maintenance of various kinds. The kinds of services provided through the association vary greatly from one community to another, an issue addressed in Chapter 8.

Finally, downsizing requires de-cluttering, and at the end of the process there will be fewer things to maintain. Economists have pointed out that consuming more goods—more furnishings, more electronic gadgets, and more "labor-saving" appliances—requires more input of our time and effort to maintain and service those consumer goods. Think of the time you spend waiting for repair persons to arrive or tinkering with your electronic gadgets to get them to work properly. If you downsize your collections of knickknacks and books, there is even less dusting (or at least less dust!) We will address de-cluttering in the next few chapters, but don't wait until then to get started. Tackle a closet, a kitchen drawer, or a bookshelf in the meantime!

Assignment: Your Information Team

In addition to making a list of questions and starting con-versations with friends, family, and neighbors, you need to find a resource team. Once you get involved in the process of deciding and transitioning, you will need a group of pro-fessionals who can help you with information, analysis, and transition. Some of your conversations with family and friends will be about referrals for this team, because good profes-sional help can make a huge difference in terms of finances, good choices, and peace of mind.

In the last chapter you identified your emotional support team: people who can help you through the emotional tran-sition from the way things are to the way things are going to be, including working through grief over losses and looking forward to positive changes. Identifying your information team is the assignment for this chapter. You should start by creating a list of the kinds of help you need. Then put the name of a person or organization next to each need. This person should be experienced in the field you've assigned him or her to, trustworthy, and available. Your information team can also help you identify people who can help you through the other half of the transition, the problem-solv-ing, decision-making part. Some people may help you with both information gathering and decision-making.

If you are staying put, you will want to talk to experts in retrofitting your home and repurposing some of the spaces. If you are going to relocate, you will need help exploring the financial options, navigating the process of selling and buying a home, deciding how much to invest in your current home to prepare it for sale, and then hiring people to get it ready. You will also need help finding a new home, disposing of some of your possessions at the best possible price, making sure you have the necessary legal documents, investing the profits (if any) from your current home, and making repairs or improvements to the new home. You will work with Realtors, representatives of your new community, bankers, financial advisors, attorneys, contractors, and people who do repair work. There is a tremendous amount of information to acquire and process, so don't be afraid to reach out for the help you need.

There may be community resources to help you start thinking your way through the options and the decision-making process. Educational programs for seniors frequently offer lectures or workshops on issues related to housing, finances, downsizing, and lifestyle changes. See what is available in your community. These programs can give you a chance to learn from the experience and insight of those who have either been through the process themselves or have helped others through the process of downsizing.

PART III

De-Cluttering: Getting Rid of Stuff

Four

Working Through
the Clutter

*A journey of a thousand miles begins
with but a single step.* Lao-Tze

Likewise, disposing of a thousand things begins with but a single item. A small first step puts you on the road to an uncluttered life, and, for most of us, thinking of big changes in small increments makes the journey much less daunting. Two of Holley's daughters, for example, are runners. They run half-marathons, which are just over 13 miles, but they both started with short jogs and worked their way up. You can tackle de-cluttering in the same way, starting small and eventually building up a full head of steam.

Actually, there are four preliminary steps to de-cluttering. Number one is motivation (incentives and rewards), which we dealt with in Chapter 2. The second step is to confront the primary avoidance strategy: when we face overwhelming clutter, the inclination is to add more space instead of subtracting possessions. This solution, obviously, is a band aid, not a cure. The third step is to change your habits—this means both ridding yourself of unhelpful habits and establishing better ones in their place. The fourth and final preliminary step is to explore your relationship with stuff, because stuff may be what is keeping you from getting started. In Chapter 2 we addressed the issue of motivation from the perspectives of overcoming obstacles and enjoying the benefits of de-cluttering. Chapter 4 explores the remaining three steps that can launch you on your journey: tackling the storage option, figuring out how to change your habits, and thinking about your relationship to stuff.

Remember the quote from Steven Covey in the last chapter? As you begin de-cluttering, keep the end in mind. The end is a house free of clutter, attractive, comfortable, and accessible, so you can find things when you need them. It is also a house that will be easier to leave if you decide to downsize.

Step Two: More Storage Space is (usually) Not the Answer

Think back to our discussion of voluntary simplicity in Chapter 2. "Less is more" is obviously a minority view in our consumer-oriented culture, which is constantly assuring us that more is better. If you took economics in college, "more is better" was one of the basic assumptions that was never questioned. Obviously, there are plenty of things in our lives for which more is not better—noise, pollution, congestion, litter—and clutter. But for many people, acquiring more possessions—the novelty of a new car or a new TV, the pleasures of shopping, wearing the latest fashion—is considered a good thing, even if you have nowhere to put these new acquisitons. If those possessions crowd the available space, the answer must be more space.

The size of the average American new home grew from 1,400 square feet in 1970 to 2,700 square feet in 2009. The storage locker rental business is booming, and pods come to rest in some backyards for indefinite periods to house the overflow of stuff. But more stuff and more space demand more of our time and attention. We have to take care of it, or sometimes it just takes time to find what we are looking for in all that stuff. It's also expensive to rent a locker or a pod, and over time the rental cost will probably exceed the value of the contents.

Look at it this way. One toaster is good. If you have a guest apartment, two toasters might be marginally better. But three? Or five? They are just in the way, and they don't improve our lives in any particular way. Most of us can only use one toaster, one washing machine, one refrigerator at a time (okay, maybe a small one in the rec room…).

In order to persuade us to buy more gadgets, sellers have to make them more specialized. You may have only one refrigerator, but computers? A typical computer user has a desktop, a laptop, a tablet maybe, and a smart phone. They do different things. The desktop is multipurpose and attached to a printer, but it is not portable. The tablet travels easily and doubles as a camera, as does the smart phone. The laptop is handy on the road for giving presentations and for writing, which the tablet doesn't do very well.

Electronics is just one kind of clutter. Kitchen equipment is equally prone to proliferation. There are specialized knives, pots and pans, and small appliances that are only for chopping eggs, or draining pasta, or spinning lettuce. It takes a lot of kitchen storage to have every possible piece of equipment for everything you might decide to cook. We are reluctant to let a gadget go because we "might need it." A good rule for gadgets, clothing, and other household items is: if you haven't touched it, viewed it, worn it or used it in a year—toss it!

Holley and Carl both had home offices after the chil-dren grew up and no longer needed their bedrooms. Carl complained constantly that his office was too small. The two offices were actually the same size, but he had two large desks instead of one, and he never threw anything away. Cleaning out his office led to the discovery that, in addition to his desktop computer, he also owned six laptops, including several he didn't know he had. The more stuff he accumulated, the less able he was to find anything, and if he couldn't find it, he bought another. His bookshelves contained more than 20 years of National Geographic Magazine, and his closet contained 36 slide carousels. As a result, his office was indeed too small. In the long run, it usually makes more sense to scale down the number of possessions than to expand the space needed to house them.

So the first question you have to ask yourself is, do I really want to solve my clutter problem by creating more storage space, or should I try to solve it by reducing the volume of stuff to be stored? Or perhaps, can I use my existing storage space more effectively and efficiently to store what I already have? The answer that works for you may be a combination of all three, but it's cheaper and ultimately more satisfying to use the existing space better, both by storing more efficiently and by storing less stuff. It's cheaper because storage space—adding on to the house, a shed, a rental storage unit—is expensive. It's more satisfying because you will know what you have and where it is when you need to use it. If you are considering downsizing, the storage issue is even more important, because you are likely to have less storage space in your next home than you have now.

Step Three: Trading Old Habits for New Habits

What are the habits that result in clutter and perpetuate the boxes, bags, piles and dust-catchers that keep you from enjoying the possessions that are truly useful, valuable, and/or meaningful to you? What kinds of habits can you develop that will reverse this pattern?

Sometimes we have to de-clutter in a hurry. That haste and old habits can lead to some bad decisions, like throwing away things that we should keep or creating boxes and bins of clutter to be dealt with at a later date. If you know that you will be moving sometime in the future, but not next month, you have the chance to begin the process now and de-clutter in a more leisurely, effective, and satisfying way. That good process begins with cultivating good habits.

In order to eliminate clutter, we must dispose of some possessions and organize the rest. This requires changing some of our habits. Changing habits is not easy. It demands awareness and intentionality and mental effort. Much of our day-to-day activity is on autopilot, so changing habits means reprogramming the autopilot. Estimates of how long it takes to eliminate a bad habit or develop a new one vary, depending on the source and the nature of the habit, but three weeks is a widely cited minimum. Changing a habit means waking up every morning and reminding your autopilot brain that you are going to do something differently today.

Changing habits also requires motivation and rewards. Once you start making visible progress on de-cluttering, the new habit becomes its own reward, because life is more present, your home is more attractive, and you can find things when you need them. But in the interim, it's a good idea to program in some small prizes for your good efforts. You may reward yourself with time alone in the back yard just reading and listening to the birds. It may be a cup of tea or a tiny piece of dark chocolate, a phone check-in with a good friend, reading a magazine, or putting your favorite CD on for a good listen. As long as the reward isn't going shopping for more stuff, reward away!

You may want to practice changing habits with something very small. Fran recommends reprogramming your landing zone. The landing zone is the place where you drop everything when you walk in the door. It may be the dining room table if it's convenient, or the kitchen counter. That space becomes a clutter magnet. Suppose you choose just a few items that come into the house every day—your keys, the mail, the newspaper. Where do they go, and how long do they stay there?

Here are some simple practices that might work for you. Put the keys in your purse or on a key rack near the door. After reading the newspaper, put it directly into the recycling bin. (Convenient access to the recycling bin is a very important dimension of de-cluttering!) The mail is often the hardest challenge. Junk mail can go directly to recycling, bills to the desk for paying, and magazines in the magazine basket. Those three categories cover most of the mail, since today's personal correspondence usually arrives in the form of email—another form of clutter that we will address in the final chapter.

Fran offers two great suggestions for habits that will develop greater pride in order and appearance, pride that will inspire you to put forth greater efforts to make your house attractive and functional. Both habits are very simple, and both reflect her experience as an extension agent and Realtor. One habit is to make the bed every day. It does wonders for the appearance of the bedroom, it takes very little time (if it takes a lot of time, you may want to rethink your bed coverings!), and a neat bed is much nicer to climb into at night. The other good habit is to "close the kitchen" before going to bed. Clean the dirty dishes, wipe down the counter and sink, put a dish towel over the front of the sink, and make it clear to family members that the kitchen is closed until morning. You can do these two tasks yourself, or you can assign them to another family member who is willing to make that one small contribution.

In addition, you may have or want to develop other habits that will help maintain the order and appearance of your home. Some families do a group five minute pickup of the family room or living room, putting toys, clothes, books, and papers where they belong. Others assign particular tasks to particular family members to keep an eye on a clutter hot spot, making sure that everyone in the family has some assignment, however small. Even a young child can put away toys or shoes.

Another step on the 1,000 object journey to de-cluttering is to develop the habit of addressing clutter in some specific way every day. The exact form of this habit will vary from person to person, depending on your time constraints and your personality type. Fran suggests setting a timer for 15 minutes (you can buy a cheap timer, or use the one on your stove or microwave) and tackling a task like kitchen or dresser drawers until the bell dings. Then you can pat yourself on the back and give yourself a reward. If you have become absorbed in the task, or are close to finishing, you can always set the timer for another 10 or 15 minutes.

Holley prefers to address de-cluttering by the numbers or the category of objects rather than time. Today the area may be books, which is a major personal challenge. The task is to identify 10 books to recycle to the used book store or friends who might enjoy them or the library or the church book sale. The books go into a bag and into the car to be delivered sometime on the daily rounds. Tomorrow the task might be cleaning out two photo albums or a kitchen drawer, or it might be giving 10 items of clothing to Goodwill. When it's done, it's done, and there is no need to think about de-cluttering again until tomorrow. You may have another way of developing daily de-cluttering habits that work for you. Just remember that when you are trying to change habits, don't take on more than a few at a time. It takes time, energy, and attention to change habits, and, if you take on too many habits at once, you are setting yourself up for failure.

Another technique that may help you change habits is to enlist your support system. Tell a friend or two what you are doing. They may have habits of their own they are working on. You can check in periodically with each other, celebrate your small successes, confess and forgive yourself for your occasional failures. We all do better at "being good" when someone else is watching!

Step Four: Me and My Stuff, A Love Story

The final preliminary step in getting ready to de-clutter is exploring your relationship to material possessions. Why do you keep certain things and discard, donate, or recycle others? What is it about specific objects, or possessions in general, that gets in the way of gaining control over clutter? If you can be more aware of how you relate to possessions, what leads you to acquire them and why you are reluctant to let go, then you will have eliminated an important hurdle on your journey to a clutter-free life.

If you have ever watched the reality show *Hoarding: Buried Alive* on the Learning Channel, you have probably witnessed a pathological attachment to something most people would classify as trash—old newspapers, broken furniture, empty containers. Perhaps you respond with relief that you aren't nearly that bad. But chances are, there is also a flitter of recognition of your own behavior, of things you should let go of but don't. If you aren't de-cluttering because it is too much work, then your main challenge is to work on the habits we have just discussed and will expand on in the next chapter. But, if you are holding on to things for other reasons, then it's time to have a serious conversation with yourself and/or your family members about keepers and shedders and the difference between them, and about letting go.

What are your treasures? What really matters? How do you let go? The answers to these questions are very different for someone who lives alone versus someone with one or more resident family member. But even if you share your space with a hoarder, the journey of 1,000 steps or 1,000 objects best begins with you. Several members of our focus groups admitted that they had not done nearly enough de-cluttering when they downsized and had to deal with surplus stuff after they moved. Several years later, they still had stuff in storage or piles of boxes that they had not yet addressed. While you may be tempted to put it off, it is easier and less expensive to dispose of clutter before moving than after.

Strategies: Visions for Each Room

Before making decisions about specific objects, it is extremely helpful to construct a big picture. This comes naturally to those who are Ns on the Myers-Briggs scale, but it's important for the detail-oriented Ss as well to step back and create a context for their choices. What is your vision for each room? What are the important activities that take place there, and, within the room, what activities need a specific zone (dressing, reading, preparing meals, watching television, etc.)?

Most rooms serve several purposes. The furnishings, storage, equipment, and décor in your big picture all need to be chosen and arranged to serve those purposes. Then, as you start the de-cluttering process, you can look at specific items and ask if they move you closer to or father away from that vision.

Strategies: Hide and Decide

Some things we keep because they are useful. Be careful with that justification, though. It is easy to assume that certain possessions are useful when in fact they are seldom if ever used. One trick to determine if something is useful is to put it in some kind of temporary storage in the garage or attic and make a date to revisit it in six months. If you haven't used it in six months (Christmas decorations don't count!), then perhaps it is time to let it go. The same applies to clothing. If you haven't worn something lately, put it in a spare closet and revisit it next year, allowing for a full cycle of the seasons. If it hasn't migrated back to your regular closet in a year, chances are you won't go looking for it in the future.

Not every possession lends itself to this "hide and decide" method, but it's good for kitchen and clothing and possibly other categories of possessions as well. So as you tackle various de-cluttering projects, this trick may provide a transition strategy for items in that middle category between keep and dispose. (If you cringe when you read the word "dispose," you probably have some work ahead of you, but don't despair. The next chapter helps with strategies for disposal.)

Strategies: BOOGO

Lots of stores offer buy one, get one free—BOGO for short. While this type of marketing is meant to entice you to buy an extra shirt, two packages of socks, or an extra pound of coffee, think before you succumb to the temptation. Over time, BOGO can clutter your closets and shelves. An antidote to BOGO is BOOGO—buy one, one goes out. If you have enough shoes, then adding a new pair requires that you recycle or discard a pair from your closet. The same rule applies to t-shirts, blouses, underwear, and most of the wearables in your house. Books are another candidate for a BOOGO policy, unless you plan to keep adding bookshelves. Electronics, too, need to be recycled when you decide to upgrade. Decide what kinds of purchases require a BOOGO policy. It obviously doesn't apply to coffee or toilet paper, because they will be used up in due time. It's the stuff that stays around and accumulates siblings and cousins that generates clutter.

Strategies: Thanks for the Memories

Other items that are difficult to let go of are those that carry memories. Photographs and heirlooms are special categories that are dealt with in the next chapter, but as you look around your house, you will probably see many other items that are associated with the person who gave them to you or the place you were visiting when you bought them. People give us gifts that we might not have chosen for ourselves. It may be hard to find a gracious way to let it go, especially if this person visits your home frequently, but souvenirs can accumulate to the point where you don't see any of them because there are too many. You simply need to explain that downsizing is limiting your space.

Line up groups of these possessions, room by room, and sort them into four categories: high in cash value and rich in memories, high value but low emotional content, low value but high emotional content, and low in both cash value and sentimental value. The last category goes into the removal station in your car or garage. Items with market but not sentimental value should be sold or donated for maximum benefit. It's the first and third categories that require some serious decision making. Items that have sentimental meaning, both those that are worth something in the market and those that are not, may carry some of the same memories for other family members or friends. Perhaps they would like to have some of these items. Choose a limited number of these that you want to keep and then try to sell or find good homes for the others. We will talk more about specific strategies for disposal in the next chapter.

Strategies: De-Cluttering with a Partner

If you share your living space, it may be more difficult to work out a way to declutter. Your treasures may be his (or her) trash. You probably have different personality traits that make the two of you approach de-cluttering differently. Imagine someone who makes calculated decisions and makes them quickly and has no regrets letting go, but she is married to someone who is sentimental about objects and slow to decide. Left alone, the calculating and prompt person may discard things that should be kept, so the constraint of her partner may result in a better process. Left alone, the person of sentiment and lack of haste may never get around to de-cluttering without some prodding. So the two need to have a conversation about setting time limits and goals in the de-cluttering process, and compromises must be made between two styles that respect the value of differences.

Perhaps the easiest place to start is with your own stuff, inviting your partner to do the same. If that doesn't work then it is time to find a second strategy. Here are some possibilities:

- Go through a shelf of books or a stack of CDs or some other collection of shared objects and sort them into those to keep and those to dispose of in some way. Then invite your partner to look at the dispose pile and choose those to be kept. You may want to put a limit on the number!
- Put away a selection of items in some remote place, like the attic, garage, or basement for six weeks to three

months (date the container!). If your partner hasn't asked about it or looked for it in that time period, then it's time to open the container and make some final decisions.

- Find yourself a de-cluttering coach—a friend, a professional of some kind, or a family member who is willing and able to be objective and encouraging while keeping you both on task.
- Engage other family members in the process of disposal. Both of you may find it easier to let go of things if they are going to a good home within the family, where they will be treasured and used. More on that in the next chapter.

The opposite situation, de-cluttering after losing a partner, can be both easier and more difficult. Both Holley and Vanessa faced that situation: Vanessa, widowed at 64, and Holley, moving at age 72 after Carl was moved to a nursing home with mid-stage Alzheimer's. Dealing with the partner's stuff can be challenging, because you want his (or her) treasures to be appreciated by someone else. But it can also be easier, because there is only one person making decisions. Holley is a J on the Myers-Briggs scale, so she is much more decisive than Carl, who is a P. Each of her efforts to de-clutter earlier in their marriage had run into a dead end because Carl was unable or unwilling to decide or let go. After Carl moved to the nursing home, their daughters took many of his sailing mementos and other items that were both useful and mementos of their Dad. One member of the sailing club where Carl was active for many years made sure that his sailing gear, pictures, and other treasures went to good homes or to the annual benefit auction for Hospice. Another member took the picture framing supplies and some of the nautical photos for his mother, who had worked with Carl for many years teaching young sailors basic sailing skills. A son-in-law took many of Carl's tools after carefully making up a toolbox for Holley for basic household tasks.

For Vanessa, grief was mixed with relief as she went through the process of downsizing and de-cluttering. Disposing of her late husband's tool clutter and replacing some of the decorating choices that had come about through compromise with rugs and pictures more to her own taste was a bittersweet experience. Family members gladly claimed many of the possessions, and others were sold as Vanessa downsized from 3,400 square feet on two stories to 2,000 square feet on a single level.

Strategies: Moving an Aging Parent or Dealing with a Parent's Estate

Many of the participants in our focus groups had dealt with downsizing and de-cluttering, not for themselves, but for a parent or grandparent. This kind of de-cluttering can be as difficult, if not more so, than facing your own treasures. Some had moved an aging parent to a nursing home or assisted living facility and were faced with the task of downsizing someone else's stuff with varying degrees of participation by the elderly parent and other family members. It's always hard to deal with another's prized possessions, whether they are present for the de-cluttering process or not, because we want to treat loved ones and their possessions with respect. Furniture is relatively easy to let go of through sale or donation, while photos and heirlooms are the hardest. (We address that issue in the next chapter.) Those who had been through the process of downsizing a parent or dealing with a parent's estate described it as daunting, difficult, and ultimately satisfying. Most of them also experienced it as a wakeup call to start dealing with their own clutter and planning for their own future downsizing.

May held a family auction to raise funds to pay the expenses for her mother in a nursing home. Jane put prices on everything and let people bid, with the money taken out of their inheritance rather than paid in cash. Arthur hired a young person to help with selling valuables and paid her a 50 percent finder's fee. He was helped by the thoughtfulness of his mother, who had gone to the trouble of creating a notebook of valuable items to help with disposal—when and where acquired and the purchase price. Anyone with an aging parent, or those of us who have become aging parents, might consider doing this simple thing as a gift to survivors.

Parents are not the only family members who leave us possessions to deal with. So do our children, who blithely go off to college and career and, along with the memories, leave behind the debris of 18 years of toys, books, clothes, science fair projects, and in the case of Holley's daughter, shelves of sheet music and a spider made out of bottle caps. Often our children live for a time in small quarters and regard the parental home as free storage space, but once they settle in a home of their own, firm deadlines are in order to claim their clutter.

Several focus group members admitted that they were the ones unable to let go of their children's things. Science fair projects and toys were taking up space and making downsizing difficult. Their children didn't want them. Holding onto childhood memories is good, but memories don't need to be attached to objects. Taking photos and either tossing or giving usable toys to those who can use them are ways to preserve the memories and enjoy thoughts of the children who get to use those toys now.

Assignment: Getting Started

The assignment for this chapter consists of choosing the habits you are going to change or develop and starting with just one or two. What small positive changes will you make in your house—handling the mail, or committing to make the bed or close the kitchen? How will you get started de-cluttering with a small but manageable daily assignment—a time commitment, a commitment to dispose of a certain number of things, or a space to be addressed like a shelf on the bookshelf, a kitchen drawer or cabinet, or a couple of dresser drawers? If you have a partner, how will you engage him or her in this effort so that there is mutual support rather than conflict over de-cluttering?

So enter these three steps in your notebook. First, take one or more of the small positive habit-forming steps that are mostly about reminding yourself of your commitment. Second, choose the form of your daily assignment for de-cluttering, along with a list of the daily assignments for at least the next week. Third, have a conversation with your partner, if you have one, about how you are going to proceed in this effort with mutual respect, affection, and love.

Five

Disposing of Stuff

Out of, say, 123 people I've talked to about letting go of all sorts of stuff – material and emotional – 88% of them wished they'd done it sooner, and 97% of them have no regrets whatsoever. Only 3% are still confused. When you let go, the odds are in your favour.
–Danielle LaPorte

The process of de-cluttering can't be separated from where the "stuff" is going. It's easier to part with prized possessions, just like kittens and puppies, if you know they are going to a good home. This chapter helps you explore some of the traditional and innovative ways to send your surplus or expendable stuff on its journey. We also address some special challenges—photographs, books, memorabilia, heirlooms, paper, and hazardous wastes.

Some of your excess stuff will, inevitably, find its way to the landfill. But that's the last resort. There is stuff that carries meaning and memory, stuff that is useful as it is or to someone else in a transformed way, stuff that can be sold, stuff that will make someone else happy. To the extent that we can reduce the volume of our material possessions in ways that offer the satisfaction of helping someone else, preserving memories, generating income for some other purpose, or recycling it in ways that provide the raw material for something new, there is less pain and more joy in letting go.

When it comes to figuring out what to do with your stuff, you have three basic choices beyond the landfill. You can sell it; you can give it to others; or you can keep it. If you keep it, you can continue to use it as you've been using it, or you can put it to a different use. The motto of the waste reduction movement is reuse, recycle, reduce. Reuse is everything from saving plastic grocery bags to carry your lunch to work to using cloth bags at the grocery store to re-using gift wrap to printing on the other side of used printer paper. It also includes repurposing. A small dresser from the bedroom, for example, could become storage in the bathroom, or a place to keep CDs and DVDs.

Cities and counties have made recycling easier by developing recycling centers where materials can be extracted and reused, including old television sets, metal objects of all kinds, and even roof shingles and used oil. Check your local recycling center for a list of things that they will take and reuse rather than put in the landfill. If you take your trash to a recycling center where it can be run through a compactor, even the landfill will be less burdened with your stuff. Reuse and recycle are two of the more satisfying ways to reduce, and de-cluttering is all about reducing.

How do you work through your stuff? This question is one of personal style, but there are a few general principles that work for almost everyone. First, if you have some lead time, start with something manageable. Clean the kitchen drawers, or the bedroom closet, or a bookcase, or the bathroom cabinets. The satisfaction you get from improvements in a defined area will encourage and inspire you to tackle the harder places.

Second, enlist help—a spouse, a child or grandchild, a friend, or even an organizing professional. They will keep you working, make it more fun, and help you deal with the emotional side. Third, celebrate your accomplishments as you go, and be kind to yourself. Clutter wasn't accumulated overnight, and it's going to take time, effort, and energy to get it under control.

Choosing What to Keep

The hardest part of de-cluttering is sorting possessions into keepers and non-keepers. The non-keepers will in turn be sorted into items to sell, to give away, and to recycle or discard. Sometimes it is easier to let go of a potential keeper if you know it is going to a person who will cherish it as you did, either because they are a friend or family member who appreciates the personal history of an item, or because of the price that person is willing to pay for it. So your first cut is not just keep/don't keep, but the more complicated options of keep, sell or give to someone particular, donate, and trash.

It helps to make the keeper/non-keeper decision with your space in mind. If you are downsizing, where will the item go in your new space? This question is especially important for furniture. If you have already identified the new space, you need to measure. Eyeball estimates of the size of the furniture and the size of the space are notoriously unreliable. Find or buy a good tape measure, and keep it with you.

We keep items for two reasons: usefulness or sentiment. We need furniture, kitchen equipment, tools, linens, clothing, books—we probably just don't need as much! So a starting point is to decide which things you actually use —how many towels and sets of sheets, which pots and pans, how many glasses and sets of dishes, how many shelves of books (once you have decided about bookshelves, that puts a limit on books). Sometimes less sentimental items are the easiest place to start. Just empty out a linen closet or the dish shelves of your kitchen and think about what you use, how many to keep, and stack the rest somewhere to decide the best way to give it a good sendoff.

Sentiment is a more nebulous guide because it is less rational than usefulness. Sentiment tends to compete with space in deciding what to keep and what to let go. Some sentimental items (souvenirs, pictures, and heirlooms) are treasures we want around us as long as possible, regardless of our space constraints. Be sure you know where they are going to be put in the new space and how many items you can accommodate. It is almost inevitable that there will be a second winnowing after you move, but do as much as you can before moving. Some "keepers" may be earmarked for a particular recipient when you are gone (some people actually label those items!) or offered to a friend or relative now.

Finally, there is paper. Some paper is kept for sentimental reasons, like the letters Holley's great-grandfather wrote to her great-grandmother back east when he was homesteading in Kansas. But much of our paper clutter is record keeping, held onto because we are not sure what we need to keep or how to dispose of it safely. The topic of record keeping is a pretty specialized one. The next chapter offers a few observations and suggestions and point you to some specialized resources about home record-keeping.

What's it Worth? Selling Your Surplus Goods

Figuring out what is worth selling and then pricing it for sale is an art form. Most of us think our possessions (including our homes!) have much more market value than they really do. So we need someone (like a prospective buyer, or an objective friend or professional) to provide a reality check. We also need to decide how long we are willing to wait for a good price rather than accept a quick sale. Even if you are not using the internet as a sales tool, it can be a good resource for estimating prices. eBay is particularly good for that purpose. As a rule of thumb, used items in good condition generally sell for 25 to 35 percent the original price, but it varies greatly from item to item. Collectibles are the most difficult to price. That's where a consignment seller or a dealer who will buy it for resale may be your best option.

For most people 55 or older, familiar traditional methods of selling household items to others include word of mouth (I have a good used bicycle, if you know anyone who wants to buy one), dealers (especially for antiques and collectibles), auctions, yard sales, classified ads in the newspaper, or signs on the drugstore window. Classified ads have gone modern in that they are not only in the newspaper but also posted online. There are also free newspapers that take ads on various terms, usually a fee, sometimes for a percentage of the price.

If you are interested in putting some items up for auction, look up auction firms in your area at Auctionzip.com. With an auction, you can set a minimum acceptable price. The auctioneer will get the best price possible, because his fee is a percentage of the price. Some auctions are general, but many specialize in antiques and collectibles. Dealers will usually buy items from you directly at a price that is negotiated, but typically 50-60 percent the likely retail price. Consignment shops will help you to set a price and take a percentage, typically 20 percent of the sales price. You will be asked to agree to both an initial asking price and a minimum price. Some consignment shops reduce the price at intervals in order to move more merchandise, but this is part of the agreement with the seller.

The multifamily yard sale or flea market divides the work and provides support. Asking prices are generally in the range of 20-30 percent of the original price for items in good condition. Many communities organize flea markets or yard sales to attract more customers and share the advertising cost. See if your community has such a program or might be willing to start one.

Consignment sales events, particularly for children's clothing, toys, and furnishings, which are quickly outgrown, are also springing up in many places. Consignment shops are increasingly popular, especially for clothing and furniture. These older sales forums still work, but they can be haphazard and time consuming. Often a great deal of effort goes into a yard sale, along with some expense for advertising, with a relatively low return both in cash and in items disposed of. Consignment sales are somewhat easier, but the seller does take a substantial cut of the price.

More recently, new variants on these traditional methods of selling surplus stuff have evolved. Younger people who have grown up with the internet are more familiar with the use of media to sell items. eBay is probably the most famous for larger items. Amazon.com and other sites buy used books, CDs, and videos. You can become an authorized seller on amazon, but you can also just sell to amazon and other sites directly, which is easier but doesn't net nearly as much money. There are web sites specializing in clothing (in general, or by age, gender, or variety, including vintage clothing), such as closetdashshop.com or crossroadstrading.com. Some sites buy items from you, while others charge a fee per item sold, send you the proceeds, and either return unsold items to you (you pay shipping) or donate them to charity. Craigslist is another possibility. About.com recommends that you sell on Craigslist if you only have a few pieces to sell and the value is medium to high (at least $20 per item).

If you don't have the time or the internet savvy to use either traditional or internet methods, you might hire a young person to work for you on commission. It's great part-time work for a high school or college student, especially a young relative. Having someone to work with makes the task of disposal easier and more enjoyable, and it provides a second set of eyes and ears to identify what might be valued by others.

Giving Stuff Away: Family First

If you are reluctant to part with items for sentimental reasons but have more stuff than fits well in your space, it is time to give things away. There are three choices: family and friends, strangers (Freecycle and its relatives), and charity. Generally we start with family and friends, especially for heirlooms and memorabilia, because it is typically easier to give our treasures to loved ones than to complete strangers, even if they are in need.

If you have grown children who are still storing possessions at your home, you have to deal with that issue first. Their clutter must be transferred to their space, and you need to set a clear deadline for this to occur. When Holley's middle daughter moved to New Jersey and finally had her own place with plenty of storage, it was time to pack up 22 boxes of her daughter's possessions and shipped them north, a few at a time so her daughter could sort them at a leisurely pace. It took 15 years from the time Holley and Carl's last child went to college until the last of the children's possessions left home, but by the time they were ready to downsize, everything that was left belonged only to Holley and Carl.

Everyone's family situation is different. Some of us have many close relatives and have to negotiate who gets what. Others have little or no family and are concerned about where their prized possessions will end up, especially heirlooms and memorabilia. If you have family, you need to consult them about what they want. You may be surprised! Holley's unloved Jasper Johns print was welcomed by her oldest daughter, an artist. For sentimental reasons, the middle daughter wanted something her Dad had made. She ended up taking two end tables Carl had built. All three daughters competed for their father's sailing trophies, which combined sentiment and practicality, because the sailing club trophies were etched glass salad bowls, pitchers, mugs, and other eating accessories.

A family gathering is one way to showcase available items, but if that's not practical, taking photos can help. In this digital age it is easy to photograph objects with a smart phone or tablet and email the photo to potential recipients to determine who wants what. Some people invite family members to put a tag on certain objects they want, so when they are ready to part with them, whether now or after they are gone, there is less uncertainty. Others respond to requests for particular items, trying to make sure that everyone gets a chance to ask for their favorites.

As Fran's mother-in-law was downsizing, she enlisted her children in her de-cluttering process in a unique and successful way. She invited them to come to her home and choose what they wanted, but she told them they had to get it out within two weeks, either taking it with them or arranging to have it shipped. This requirement limited their appetites for family heirlooms, especially large ones, but it got the job done. At the end of her life, she had reduced her cherished possessions to a carload of items—and the car wasn't even an SUV!

Diane had the opposite problem—she had no one to leave things to. An only child, she inherited the treasures of both sides of her family. She and her husband recently moved into a two bedroom townhouse in a retirement community, and after more than two years, there are still many unpacked boxes sitting in their dining room. They have two children. The son is married and has a son, but none of them is interested in family treasures. The daughter is divorced and lives in a small apartment. The meaning and memories that are carried by the family possessions have nowhere to go. Diane's choices are limited. Some items may find a home in a local museum. Other items may be sold, or given away, or left for her children to deal with. In the meantime, there are all those unpacked boxes in Diane's dining room that are keeping her from enjoying her new home. The emotional impact of feeling like "the end of the line" is also keeping her from getting on with her new life, but it's too difficult for her to deal with right now.

Giving Stuff Away: Freecycle and its Relatives

Freecycle is one of several websites where you can post both what you have to give away and what you are looking for. Freecycle operates in a local area, so the people on the list are all within driving distance. An interested person contacts you directly, usually by email, and you can arrange for that person (or one of several) to pick up the items. You may have a choice of recipients. Especially popular on Freecycle are baby equipment, toys, and furniture

Moving boxes are a popular Freecycle item; Fran gave hers to someone moving from South Carolina to Montana, to the same town where her son was living. Holley gave a glider to someone who turned out to be working at a factory owned by her husband's cousin. She threw in some Loony Tunes wall hangings with a sofa for a family with a new baby whose room needed decorating. No money was earned, but Fran and Holley both received the satisfaction of helping someone.

Because items on Freecycle are free, the process can be frustrating. Do be cautious about inviting strangers into your home, and expect that people who accept enthusiastically may fail to show up (after all, it's free!) or be looking for items to resell. But it's not a bad way of matching what you no longer want to a particular person who needs just that item.

One of Holley's best experiences with Freecycle was Carl's collection of National Geographic magazines, described in an earlier chapter. On Freecycle, three different families with home-schooled children wanted them for projects! Sometimes Freecycle is the inspiration to give away something you hadn't even thought about. Someone posted a request on Freecycle for tiger lilies, for example, and Holley's needed culling. The next day, a man showed up with his wife, two buckets, and a shovel.

Giving Stuff Away: Charitable Donations

If you donate items to a 501c(3) corporation, you can take a tax deduction for your contribution. A 501c(3) corporation is one to which you can make deductible contributions either in cash or in kind. Churches, schools and colleges, nonprofit service organizations like soup kitchens and homeless shelters, arts organizations, hospitals, and groups that work with animals are just some of the examples of entities that might be interested in your excess stuff. Many operate thrift shops for resale, including the big national Goodwill chain, which helps handicapped people prepare themselves for employment. Some will pick up your larger items, especially furniture. You will need to ask for a receipt and set a reasonable value. Goodwill (www.goodwill.org) offers a handy valuation guide for many clothing and household items.

Like other ways of passing stuff on, donating to charitable organizations give you a good feeling. You are helping the organization in its good work, and you are making the stuff available to someone, probably low-income, who needs what you are giving away enough to pay some small price for it. It's also easy. Many charities have donation boxes where you can drop things off, if you don't need a receipt.

Some organizations sponsor silent auctions or yard sales as fundraisers. Many of them will provide tax receipts, especially for more valuable items. Check with some of your local organizations to see if they have such events, and ask them to notify you when one is coming up.

Assignment: Your Disposal Plan

Below is a six-step disposal plan. The steps can be taken by room, by category of object, or by any other system that works for you. The easiest is probably room by room. In each room, step one is to decide what you want to keep (or set aside to consider keeping). In the room-by-room system, this step will be repeated over and over as you work through your many rooms and storage spaces. You will probably revisit your keeper pile in each room at least once to further cull the pile of possessions once you realize that you haven't de-cluttered enough.

You have now created a collection of items you are willing to let go, so you are ready for the next step. Step two is to decide what to sell, what to give to a family member, what to donate, what to recycle, and what to throw away. You might start by color coding items with dots to identify the four categories. The trash leaves first. If you have some undecided items, set them aside and move on with the task. Revisit that pile later.

Step three is to establish a sales plan. Which items go to a dealer, which to an auction, eBay, the yellow pages, a consignment shop, a flea market, or a yard sale? The last two may be easier if you partner with friends and neighbors.

Step four is to engage your family and friends in the distribution process. This process, which we discussed earlier, allows them to choose what they want and ensures a fair distribution of the family heritage and other valuable items.

Step five is giving away. Here you have several choices, and you will probably use more than one of them if you are giving away different kinds of objects. Items can be donates to charity, given away on Freecycle, or even passed along at a free yard sale! Fran keeps a closet of wrapped objects and insists that visitors take one with them when they leave. They can do with it what they like—keep it, sell it, give it away, or throw it away. You may enjoy inventing other creative ways of giving things away.

Step six is recycling. Most of us now have access to recycling facilities, and the variety of recyclable items has expanded greatly in the last 10 years. So before you throw something in the trash, check with your nearest recycling center. It might have another life ahead of it.

After these six steps, you are left with the stuff you are keeping, whether you are moving it with you or reorganizing it in your present home. If you are moving, it is a good idea to create an inventory of the items you are keeping room by room, as professional movers do. The list may inspire you to reconsider some of your keeper/non-keeper decisions.

When you are done, take a deep breath and pat yourself on the back! You have earned a reward—so be sure to sprinkle small rewards liberally along the way.

Six

Special Challenges in De-Cluttering

Most of our troubles are due to our passionate desire for and attachment to things that we misapprehend as enduring entities. ~**Dalai Lama.**

W hen it comes to the de-cluttering process, not all items are created equal. Some items—including photographs, books/CDs/DVDs, heirlooms and memorabilia, paper, and hazardous wastes—are more challenging to deal with than others. The first three categories are loaded with memories and sentiment. They also lend themselves to the "this or that" game in deciding what stays and what goes. "This or that" is an especially useful approach if you are dealing with a partner who has trouble letting go. We have three floor lamps and only need one. Which do we keep? Which picture of the sunset? Which set of china? The last two categories, paper and hazardous waste, can overwhelm us in terms of volume and disposal challenges. This chapter offers suggestions for dealing with each of the five categories.

Photographs

Many families, including Fran's and Holley's and probably yours, have lots and lots of photographs. Slides, framed photos, albums, boxes of photos, photos on the computer. Meeting the picture challenge was the start of a two-year de-cluttering project for Holley. It was a great place to start, because photos are rich bearers of memories that can be shared and revisited, and because, when culled to a reasonable quantity, pictures become more enjoyable and valuable than they are in numbers that overwhelm. This experience was one of many for Holley that resulted in "less is more"—more enjoyment of what remained, more free space, more sharing with family and friends.

Holley started by dealing with more than 5,000 slides stored in notebooks and slide carousels, then she moved on to framed photographs, two boxes of loose photos, and 51 photo albums of various sizes and shapes. In fact, photos and books were Holley's biggest de-cluttering challenge. After going through two carousels every day for six weeks, she had culled them to about 1,000 slides worth keeping. The survivors were mostly family pictures involving children, grandchildren, travel, pets, and homes. Holley had these digitized to CDs, and she gave them to family members for Christmas. The empty carousels, which had taken up half a closet, were given away, some to friends and the rest to a church yard sale. Holley kept one carousel with the slide projector and a few very special slides.

Photos were more complicated, because there were probably 15,000 of them in frames, boxes, and albums. Holley tackled the framed family photos first. They covered the walls of the den and any available shelf space. There wasn't room for them all in the next home, so Holley culled them to current pictures and several classic family favorites from four generations.

The rest were removed from their frames and put in the sort box. The frames were donated to charity.

Holley invited one of her daughters for a weeklong visit to help jumpstart the next step of the process. Both a collector and a natural organizer, this daughter was the ideal choice to help Holley tackle the two large boxes of loose photos and 50 albums of various sizes. She helped Holley sort through many of the photos, making piles for herself, her sisters, other relatives and family friends. She made a special pile of keepers for her mother and a pile to scan to create another digitized family album. Duplicates, pictures of people and places no one recognized, and photos that made people look unattractive were especially easy to discard. Other family members—another daughter and several grandchildren—picked up where she left off, and each helper really enjoyed the old family pictures. Of all the de-cluttering projects, this one most lends itself to partnering with other family members, turning a task into an enjoyable shared experience.

Books, CDs, and DVDs

If you have ever visited the Western North Carolina home of poet Carl Sandburg, you have seen the home library to end all home libraries. The house isn't all that large, but there are bookshelves in every room and rows upon rows of them in the attic. Clearly, Carl Sandburg was not into culling his books. Holley's visit did make her feel better about her home, with its 300+ feet of bookshelves in various rooms, but the fact that books had always been Holley's most precious possession, does not free them from falling into the category of clutter.

Along with books, CDs and DVDs can be major sources of both clutter and frustration. Clutter, because each one is small and doesn't seem to add much to the pile, but all together they take over our space. Frustration, because it becomes increasingly difficult to find the book or CD or DVD you are looking for. It's also hard to choose what to read, listen to, or watch. Economist Herbert Simon coined the term "bounded rationality," which means that choice is easier when we limit the set of items among which we are choosing. Experimental studies have shown that people who are confronted with too many choices are unable to make any decision. So weeding the books, CDs, and DVDs regularly helps you to see and enjoy the blossoms in your entertainment garden.

One of the many good things about books is that there are so many people who are happy to take them off your hands. Used bookstores are a special breed of retailer: they do not do consignment, but they often offer store credit, which will, of course, tempt you to buy more books. One strategy for resisting this temptation is to take children along with you to the book store, your own grandchildren or any children you can borrow, and let them use your store credit. This way you are encouraging reading without restocking your own shelves.

You can also sell books on a number of web sites. You can donate them to the local library or thrift store. Organizations having yard sales always welcome books, knowing that they can easily dispose of leftovers. If you enjoyed the book, think of the pleasure you are passing on to someone else! During the culling process, you will rediscover books you enjoyed or treasured and want to pass them on to a family member or keep and re-read. You don't have to get rid of them all, just get them down to a manageable number. Remember, you didn't acquire them overnight, so it's okay to work through them one shelf at a time, sorting into keepers, undecided, sell and/or donate, and those to give to family members and friends. It may take two iterations shelf by shelf, filling the trunk of the car with books to go to the used book store, the yard sale at church, the library, or any other destination, but it is a rewarding experience to revisit your old friends and in the end have few enough books that you know what you have and where to find it.

Heirlooms and Memorabilia

There are two problems with disposing of heirlooms and memorabilia. The first is deciding whether they are more valuable in terms of sentiment than in terms of cash. If you decide in favor of sentiment, you face the second problem: deciding whether to keep an item or give it away. If you decide to give it away, who gets it? We offered some suggestions in the previous chapter for those who have multiple family claimants on these items. But what about the opposite problem? What do you do with your heirlooms if you have no family, or at least no interested family member?

Museums are a possible destination for items of historic value. Museums in the area where your parents lived are likely to have more interest in journals, vintage clothing, photos of places, and other possible enrichments to their collections. Vintage clothing can also be sold on a consignment basis online at several different sites.

Younger generation family members often do not want the sterling flatware, china, and crystal prized by earlier generations. If you find yourself in this situation, explore the many on-line services that purchase items so others can replace items missing from their own collections. One of those is Replacements Limited, which has both a web site and an actual store in Greensboro, NC, where you can both sell your items and buy to fill in the gaps. Obviously, if there is little or no sentiment attached to these items for you or for others, the first option is to sell them, using one of the methods described above.

If there is some historical significance to an object, you may want to explore possibilities besides family and friends. Perhaps that quilt your grandmother made belongs in a museum or cultural center. Check with museums, either locally or in the area where the heirloom or memorabilia originated. You might be surprised at how your items will fill out a collection. You may not get paid for the item, but many donations of this kind will generate a tax receipt. Before you give it away, see if your old family silver or china can be sold to companies like Replacements Limited. Likewise, vintage clothing can be sold on web sites dedicated to that purpose. So don't give up. Some of your favorite possessions may be headed for a second go-round of usefulness and attachment in a new home!

Paper

The average person spends almost an hour a day searching for lost papers, receipts, or files. In part, this number is so high because we file much more than we need to: 83 percent of things we file are never used again. Paper is a major source of clutter, because each of us has a constant flow of newspapers, junk mail, notes, cards, magazines, bills, financial statements, and other communications. The kind of paper we are concerned with here comes in two types: sentimental paper, and practical paper. Sentimental paper consists of your reports cards, diplomas, love letters, and other personal memorabilia that usually has no meaning to anyone but you. If the volume is not great, there's no harm in giving sentimental paper some space in your filing cabinet. But if it gets out of control, consider scanning some of it and saving it on a disk with a backup.

The other kind of paper is not sentimental at all. It's all those financial records and important papers. Important papers do need to be kept in a safe place—wills, passports, marriage licenses, copies of diplomas, powers of attorney—and someone else needs to know where they are and have access to them. But the financial records seem endless. How long from filing date do I need to keep records in support of my income taxes? The record of improvements to my home? All the other records and receipts I accumulate every day?

As you tackle a pile of paper, sort it into three categories: recycle, shred, and keep. It's a good idea to have a paper shredder for any paper that could result in identify theft or other compromising of your privacy, especially for financial information. The "keep" papers will need a filing system.

There are two good on-line resources that will help you set up a system for keeping and weeding financial records. One is Managing Household Records, which can be found at www.usa.gov/Topics/Money/Personal-Finance/Managing-Household-Records.shtml. The other is www.bankrate.com/finance/personal-finance/how-long-to-keep-financial-records. These two web resources should help you clear the paper clutter from your life!

What to do with the records you no longer need? There are often shredding programs in your area so that you don't have to risk identity theft by dropping your personal papers off at the recycling center. Banks, local governments, and insurance companies often have shredding programs. If you're considering investing in a personal shredder, note that home shredders are slow, so if you have access to one, the larger commercial shredder may be the way to go.

Hazardous Wastes

The last and most difficult disposal category is hazardous wastes—chemicals, paint, aerosol cans, medications, etc. Your local government can help you deal with these items. Many county or municipal governments have sites where hazardous wastes are collected or have special hazardous waste collection days. Empty paint cans are easy to dispose of, but half-full ones require special treatment. Filling them with sand or kitty litter usually solves the problem. If all else fails, take an old board and keep painting it until the can is empty! If you are having work done on your house that involves paint and other chemicals, you might enlist the aid of the contractor in figuring out how to dispose of your accumulated cans and bottles of stuff you don't want finding its way into your soil or drinking water.

Home medical waste is another challenge, particularly syringes and leftover prescription drugs. Again, check around locally for disposal programs, beginning with your local government and/or pharmacist. Many communities have a special day set aside for collecting and safely disposing of these items. You can empty your prescription bottles into a container of coffee grounds or kitty litter, seal it up, and put it in the household trash if no better solution is available. But don't flush them down the toilet. We don't need to ingest other people's prescription drugs along with our morning cup of coffee!

Assignment: Plans for Special Cases

The assignment for this chapter is to explore your options for letting go of some of the more sensitive clutter in your life, and then to try your hand at it. First, research sales and donation options for the books that no longer need space on your shelves. Remember, there are many outlets for this type of item, so this is an easy place to start.

Second, sort your heirlooms, antiques, and memorabilia according to market value and sentimental value and assign each of them to be sold, donated, or given away based on those two valuations. The sentimental value goods should be offered to family members first. If you have a larger family, you'll want to have some system for deciding who gets what. As for selling, explore the options in your area: dealers, auctions, consignment shops. Also explore on-line resources such as Craigslist, eBay, and ReplacementsLtd.

Donation possibilities are endless, depending on what kind of items you have and which charities you want to support. Higher end merchandise belongs in upscale resale shops and charity auctions, while organizational yard sales and thrift shops are more appropriate for lower end items. Some items may be directly reusable. Women's shelters, for example, need household furnishings and clothing to help women start a new life.

It will help to create a section in your notebook dedicated to an inventory of items in each category and a destination, and when your piles get to a critical mass, be sure to load them up and deliver them to their next destination.

PART IV

Choosing Your Surroundings

Seven

Envisioning Your
New Home

Where we love is home - home that our feet may leave, but not our hearts.--Oliver Wendell Holmes

This chapter explores the process of finding a home that meets your needs and desires. The question for this chapter is, what kind of living quarters do you want? Making this decision is often easier than finding the actual house. If you already live in a house, you can use it as a basis for comparison. What do you like about your present house that you would like to keep? A garage? A place for a vegetable garden? A big kitchen? And what is it that you don't like? A big yard to look after? Stairs? Outdated bathrooms? Poor lighting? Once you have looked at your present home with a critical eye, you will be better prepared to describe the home you would like to have, which is the assignment at the end of this chapter.

Take a look back at the vision you created at the end of Chapter 1 (The life you want to be living in the future). Chances are, your needs in your future home echo those expressed by the people in our focus groups—less space and yard to care for, single level, access to amenities for seniors, and close to family or friends. Most of them wanted a place in which they could grow old, something easier to manage and friendlier to declining physical abilities either now or in the future.

Interior Spaces

Houses, especially detached single-family homes, have grown dramatically in size in the last 40 years. As we noted a couple of chapters back, the average new house is almost twice as large as it was in 1970. At some point in our later years, most of us reconsider life in the mini-mansion. There is more space in our sprawling homes than we can really use, and more space means higher utility bills as well as more cleaning, maintenance, and repairs. Bigger homes are also often multilevel, and climbing stairs is likely to become a problem as we get older. So an important question to address is, how much and what kind of space do I/we need?

There is no clear or simple answer to this question. I/we may be one person, or two, or more. Expecting frequent family visitors may call for guest space, including a second bathroom. If there are two of you, and you have difficulty sharing sleeping space because one or the other snores, has insomnia, or is frequently ill. In that case, a second bedroom is a necessity, not a luxury. You may have hobbies you want to continue, or you may want space to entertain small groups of friends or relatives. An eat-in kitchen or a lot of counter space will be important to some families but not others.

Rooms and Functions

Realtors may define space in terms of square feet, but, in downsizing, you may want to start with rooms and their functions. How many bedrooms (perhaps including an office or hobby room)? How important is a single-purpose guest room rather than a guest room that is also an office, a library, or a sitting room? Do you need one bath, two, or one and a half? Do you want a separate laundry room?

How big a kitchen and living/dining room do you want? The rooms where size is most likely to matter are the living room, kitchen, and master bedroom, so at this point you do want to think about how many square feet you want in those spaces. Does the kitchen need an island? Do you need a garage or at least a place for tools, perhaps including gardening tools and supplies? Is a screened porch, patio, deck, or other outdoor living space important to you? What about light—for reading, for plants, or just because you like the feel of it? Good lighting can compensate for lack of windows and skylights, but natural lighting is important to some people.

Bart and Elaine, whom we met in Chapter 3, wanted to buy a townhouse or detached house in a particular retirement community where many of their friends lived, so their options were limited. But they had the opportunity to visit many of their friends' homes to see what worked for them. A second bedroom was important, more for sleeping apart when one of them was sick or restless than for guests. A small office would serve them both since they are fully retired, but with deteriorating eyesight, plenty of natural light was important. So was a separate dining room. Neither has much interest in gardening, and their pets are indoor cats, so yard was a minor consideration. These reflections on their friends' homes, along with their own habits and needs, helped them narrow down what they were looking for.

We are Getting Older...

We are all getting older. If you've reached or are honing in on that stage in your life when age becomes a factor in daily living, it is important to pay attention to the aspects of a potential new home's layout that relate to aging. A home on a single level with no entry stairs is generally the best choice for older people. Even if you can manage stairs now, they may not work for you in the future. Wider doorways also make the home more adaptable to mobility problems if they arise later, if mobility is not already an issue. If one person is mobility impaired, it's important that counters, cabinets, and appliances be accessible from a wheelchair. People in our focus groups who had downsized emphasized easy maintenance, at least one stall shower with a seat, and good lighting as important considerations related to aging. If the house will need alterations to fit your needs, you will need to budget for those changes.

If you are looking for a home that will be shared with other family members, from an aging parent to the family of a son or daughter, your needs will be very different than if you are going to live alone, and your options will be constrained by the needs and financial resources of the people who will share that space. In this case, you need to define your own space needs and also consider how to satisfy your need for privacy.

Karen, a widow, sold her home of more than 50 years and used part of the proceeds to help her son buy a split level with a basement that could be converted into an 800 square foot apartment with a separate entrance. She is admittedly conflicted about the outcome. Her small space is well designed to meet her needs, but, after having lived alone for quite a few years, she misses her privacy, even though she does enjoy the company of her grandson. On the other hand, she doesn't miss raking leaves and shoveling snow, because her son handles all the house and yard maintenance. It can be difficult to know how sharing space is going to work until you have already made the move.

Outdoor Space

Some but not all of your living options will come with the dreaded lawn, which demands regular mowing, and shrubbery beds, which require watering and weeding, and trees that spill their leaves every fall with predictable regularity. You have three possible responses to this outdoor maintenance challenge:

1. I love to be outdoors and plan to do my own yard chores for as long as I can.
2. I will gladly pay someone to take care of my lawn, doing a few of the tasks myself.
3. I don't need or want a lawn, low maintenance landscaping of a minimal sort is fine with me.

Even if your answer is #1, you still will want to consider a modest-sized lawn and garden when you downsize, knowing that its care will become more challenging as you get older. If you chose #2, you can probably hire someone to tend your lawn, or you can opt for a community where lawn care is included in the monthly maintenance fee. Alternatively, good landscape design can create an attractive yard with minimal maintenance requirements by avoiding grass and focusing on plants that require minimal attention. Xeriscape, for example, is a low maintenance form of landscaping with plants that don't require much water.

If your answer is #3, you may be looking for a more dense setting with houses close together and shared green space, the kinds of communities known as new urbanism. New urbanism is not limited to cities—it is found in newer development in cities and towns of all sizes. In a sense, it's an upscale return to the urbanism of the first half of the twentieth century, when our cities and towns were more walk-friendly and houses were close together to make access to shops and services easier and more convenient.

Other outdoor space might include a patio, deck, or screened porch, where you can enjoy cool mornings and evenings, cook out on the grill, and socialize with friends and neighbors. And remember, if that outdoor space is paved or covered, you don't have to mow it!

Maintenance

Houses and yards need to be maintained, and so do possessions, which is one reason de-cluttering is so important to the process of moving, particularly for older adults. Possessions are bulky and heavy; they demand our effort and attention. They need to be maintained, cleaned, serviced, and replaced. Maintenance of house, yard, and furnishings takes time and/ or money—painting, cleaning, gardening, mowing, repairs. As we grow older, and don't have children around who can take on responsibilities, we need to either reduce the volume of household chores or start paying people to do some of them. A smaller house that is designed to be low maintenance will demand less time and money. Hardwood and tile floors are easier to maintain than carpet. Windows are easier to wash if they have fewer panes and are easier to open. Think about what takes time to maintain in your present home and ways you could make those things simpler in your new home.

One financial aspect of maintenance is energy efficiency. You can get lots of good information from your local electric utility, but the house itself will have qualities that make it more or less energy efficiency. Insulation is one of them. The heating and cooling system is another. Energy Star appliances in the kitchen also contribute to saving energy. You can manage energy usage in a variety of ways, especially by controlling or programming the thermostat and using energy efficient lighting. But do plan to look critically at any prospective home from the perspective of energy efficiency.

Amenities

What do you do for exercise? Do you belong to a gym or community recreational facility? Swim? Walk or run? What about social activities? Do you like to watch movies, play bridge, or take adult lifelong learning classes? While traditional neighborhoods leave access to that kind of facilities and activities up to the individual, planned communities and especially retirement communities may have some of the facilities you want on site. Most common are fitness centers, pools, and/or walking trails. Often there are clubhouses or other facilities for hosting parties, playing bridge, viewing movies, or other community activities.

If that kind of group activity is important to you, add it to your checklist in deciding what you want in your next home. If you use exercise equipment, it makes much more sense to use shared equipment than to take up space in your smaller home with a treadmill or exercycle.

Retirement Communities

Retirement communities have come a long way from your parents' vision of the "old folks' home." Often they include the full range of housing options, from detached, single-family homes to townhouses or condominiums to independent living apartments to assisted living and skilled nursing care. Services may include access to dining facilities and transportation to shopping and cultural events. Sometimes there is an entrance fee for any access or just for assisted living and skilled nursing care.

Other retirement communities just offer a mix of detached and townhouse/condominium options with facilities and activities on site. The same mix is available from gated communities that limit outside access but are open to a full range of ages. All three usually support a fair amount of common property, green space, landscaping, and usually some indoor and outdoor recreation and services. All of them will expect you to pay dues to support the shared facilities and may periodically levy a special fee on homeowners to support repairs or new construction. As a member of the homeowners' association, you will have some voice in the fees and what they support, but your power may be limited if you are in the minority.

There may also be restrictions in the covenant that limit your ability to make structural changes, have yard signs or yard sales, or do other things that affect the appearance of your property. Pets are generally okay in owner-occupied housing (detached house, condominium, or townhouse) subject to leash laws, but they are less likely to be accepted in apartments or skilled nursing facilities.

Both retirement communities and multi-age gated communities are attracting people at an early age, many of them as early retirees and/or empty nesters. These "young old" people are generally physically and mentally active and want the facilities and programs to support that lifestyle without having to travel too far. Many of them also want to share those activities within a community of people of the same generation. If that is what you want, you will probably want to start your exploration with retirement communities.

Others prefer to stay in traditional mixed-age neighborhoods and seek programs, services, activities, and shopping outside the immediate neighborhood. They may prefer community-wide centers for recreation and exercise that bring them in contact with a broader range of ages, income levels, and backgrounds. Or they may prefer to limit their expenses by choosing amenities they can afford, rather than pay for them through homeowner association dues or other levies. Among traditional neighborhoods, there are still a lot of options, from downtown lofts (which are becoming increasingly popular) to new housing developments to older neighborhoods, where prices may be lower but maintenance may be higher and the home may need more retrofitting to adapt to your needs.

Finally, you may have a specific locational goal in your ideal retirement home. If you have mobility or vision issues, you may want to be close to public transportation or to medical facilities and shopping. If water-based recreation is an important part of your retirement plan, you probably want to explore living on or near the water. Add those items to the checklist at the end of the chapter.

Housing Options: Single Family or Multi-family?

Whether you opt for a retirement community, a gated community, or a traditional neighborhood, there are still choices within those communities. The biggest decision is whether you want a single-family, detached home or a home in a multi-family building, a townhouse, condominium, or apartment. Single-family homes usually have more freedom and more space but also more maintenance—larger yards, more interior space, and more responsibility for exterior maintenance. Usually owners of single-family detached homes in retirement or gated communities have access to any amenities, such as a pool, clubhouse, or fitness center, but this isn't always the case, so it pays to inquire.

The specific differences between townhouses and condominiums vary from state to state, but, in general, townhouse owners are responsible for maintaining the exterior of their space (excluding common areas) while condominium owners can expect the homeowners' association to take on most exterior maintenance. Condominiums usually assign more responsibilities to the homeowners' association, but that typically means higher HOA fees. You may also consider owning or renting an apartment. Owning an apartment is very similar to owning a condominium. Renting an apartment involves less responsibility and less upfront cost, but no buildup of equity and no protection against rent increases.

Financial Dimensions

Finally, there is the financial issue. There may be a gap between your housing choice and what you can afford to spend. The monthly cost is not just the mortgage payment on the house; it's also the HOA fees (in some cases) and always property taxes, insurance, utilities, and maintenance.

The price you are willing to pay will depend on how much you have available for a down payment, what interest rates you are charged, and the expected cost of any changes you want to make to your new home. If you are planning to sell your old home, there will be costs associated with getting it ready to sell, and there will be closing costs on your new home.

Mortgage calculators are available on the internet or in a number of personal financial software programs, like Quicken. You can enter the amount of the loan, the interest rate, and the duration of the loan, and the program will tell you what the monthly payment will be. Alternatively, you can enter the interest rate, the duration of the loan, and the amount of your monthly payment, and the program will tell you how much the loan would be. Add that amount to your available down payment, and you have the price you are willing to pay for your next home. It's good information to have as you start the search process in the next chapter.

Sometimes retirement communities offer help with the financial transition, and that possibility may influence your choice of where to move. We address these issues in the next chapter, but it is a good idea to start thinking now about how much you can afford each month and how much house that amount will buy.

Assignment: Describe Your New Home

You sketched out a vision at the end of Chapter 1 that included a picture of the kind of home that would fit your changing lifestyle. Your assignment for this chapter is to go back and see what you would change and what still describes what you want and need in a house.

Step 1: Make a list of what features you like about your present house that you want to have in your new home if you relocate.

Step 2: Make a list of what you don't like about your present home that you want to avoid in your new home.

For both steps one and two, be sure to address each of the issues raised in this chapter: indoor space, outdoor space, adaptation to aging, maintenance, and amenities.

Step 3: Make a list of the changes you would need to make to your present home or the features you would need in your new home to accommodate any changes that arise with aging. (Grab bars, wider doorways, accessible tub/shower, etc.)

Step 4: Taking the information in the first three steps into account, describe the home you want to live in. How close is it to the description of your present home?

Step 5: Convert the information in Step 4 to a list of things you must have and things you would like to have in your next home if you decide to move.

Eight

Where Shall I Live?

To move or not to move, that is the question. –
with apologies to William Shakespeare

Since there is nearly an endless supply of potential homes out there, it will be easier to narrow the decision of where to live next by breaking it into two steps. The first step is to weigh two "big picture" choices: stay in your present home with some modifications or move elsewhere to a house that is already better suited to your needs.

If, after careful exploration of your needs and options, you choose to stay put, that's the end of the decision-making process. But if you choose to relocate, you must then move on to consider two further options: remain in the community where you live (in a home that better suits your needs) or move away, perhaps closer to family and friends or to a milder climate, a more urban (or more rural) area, or near the mountains or on the water. Once you make it through these two big decisions, you will be ready to start either de-cluttering and remodeling (Option 1) or de-cluttering and searching for a new home (Option 2). Note that both options begin with de-cluttering.

Option 1: Staying in Place

The most compelling reason to stay put is that your current home is suitable for someone growing older, with some of the features we discussed in the last chapter—no stairs, wide doorways, grab bars, etc.—or that your home can be easily adapted to older persons. In this case, it might be a good idea to stay right where you are. Other factors may come into play, however. Is the neighborhood safe? If you can no longer drive because of problems with vision, reflexes, or disability, does your home have access to public transportation? Is it convenient to stores and services? Is there a possibility of sharing your home with other family members to help with the day to day household chores and expenses? Are you close to your neighbors, or is there family nearby? If you are answering yes to many of these questions, then you can skip most of the rest of this book and concentrate on de-cluttering and adapting your space to your present and future needs for accessibility and ease of maintenance.

In 2013, a research project at Johns Hopkins University used a team of repair people, occupational therapists and nurses to test the possibility of making inexpensive changes and developing strategies and assistance for daily living that would allow low-income older Americans to stay in their homes rather than winding up in nursing homes. Working with 800 households in Baltimore, they found that the average repairs or modifications cost only about $1,100. Wider doorways, lower toilets and kitchen counters, grab bars and ramps help people with physical disabilities to age in place. For many people, that kind of modification is the simplest and least expensive choice. While your upgrading and remodeling needs to make your home "elderproof" might be more costly than $1,100, staying put could be the least expensive alternative. Price isn't the only consideration, but it is an important part of the story.

Reasons to Stay

Sometimes people choose to stay put not because it's really where they want to be, but because it is the least expensive choice and/or involves the least effort. Financial concerns certainly constitute a valid reason, although you need to thoroughly investigate your choices before you assume that just you can't afford to move. If you have substantial equity in your home, there are ways to make a financial transition. If you don't, there are innovative ways for adapting your home to your changing needs.

When people stay put because they think it involves less effort than moving to a suitable home, they need to be mindful that it won't get any easier. If you are reasonably sure you will need a different kind of home in 10 or 20 years, remember that the process of downsizing will be even more difficult then, because you will be 10 or 20 years older. Now or then, you can be involved in the process without doing all the work yourself. You can get help, either from family and friends or from people you pay to help with the more difficult tasks. You can also spread the work over a period of time rather than doing it all at once. The earlier you begin, the easier it will be.

Drawbacks to Staying

The downside of staying put is pretty much just the flip side of reasons to stay. Your neighborhood may have changed over the years, as you have, and the home that was once a great place to raise a family and cook out with the neighbors is now a big empty space with strangers living on both sides. Your home may be multilevel and difficult to adapt to decreased mobility. Access to transportation and shopping may be limited. House and yard maintenance may be more than you are willing or able to deal with, preferring a place where someone else mows the lawn and tends the shrubs. You may be isolated from the company of others in your age range or recreational activities; you may want a community with a fitness center, walking trails, and a pool.

If your present home is not readily adaptable to the needs of someone who is elderly and infirm, then you may be facing a now or later decision. It may not be necessary that you move right now, but it is likely to be necessary in the future. Finding a home that offers some attractions and amenities that appeal to you now while also being more suited for your later years is a real investment in your future and your peace of mind.

Bear in mind that you are presently as physically and mentally able and alert as you are ever going to be, so if you are going to go through the challenge of moving, sooner will always be easier than later. If a new space is luring you with less responsibility, more congenial neighbors, and amenities you currently lack, or if you anticipate based on your own and/or your partner's health history that you will eventually need a different space, you should begin exploring the process of moving to a more appropriate home sooner rather than later.

Which will it be? Stay, de-clutter, and adapt, or look for another place to live?

Option 2: Finding a New Home

Whether you are staying in the area or relocating, your goal will be to find a number of houses in your price range that meet most of the criteria you set in the last chapter, and to choose the most nearly perfect home. Before you start reading real estate ads and calling agents, however, you need to weigh the pros and cons of staying close to home or moving farther away.

Moving Near or Far

If you like your community, if you have family and/or close friends and other ties to the community, if you like the climate and the urban or rural amenities, there is no particular reason to move elsewhere. You may have a support system, opportunities for part-time work or volunteer engagement, and social activities that will not be easy to reconstruct in a new community. People with partners may find moving easier than do people who are single, widowed, or divorced. People with family ties elsewhere will probably move with greater ease, because they are moving into a ready-made support system.

Your personality type probably figures more significantly into this decision than do more specific housing choices. Extraverts often find the adventure of moving and the opportunity to make new friends more attractive than introverts, for example. Thinking types may be more likely to calculate the costs and benefits of near versus far, while feeling types are more concerned about connections to others, both where they are now and where they are likely to seek a new home. But whatever your personality type, this decision is a big one, and it requires careful thought, information about your options, and thoughtful conversation with your partner and/or support system.

So sit down and make a list, starting with places you might like to live. Maybe you have always been attracted to the west coast, or city living, or the water. Perhaps you want a college town with sports and educational opportunities. Some people want four seasons, others prefer a more mild climate such as Florida or southern California. If cost is a factor, be sure to check out rural areas and the southern states; they typically offer the best values for your dollar. State Chambers of Commerce and Tourism Bureaus can offer lots of good information on amenities, services, options, and costs of living, like taxes and home prices. Obviously, you will want to find out what kind of housing options each place offers in the light of your "must have" list from the preceding chapter.

Narrow your choice based on what's important to you such as family ties, climate, or amenities, and then schedule visits to the places on your short list. Searching for a good place to retire to is a great way to travel, even if in the end you decide to stay right where you are.

When the time came to retire, Fran and Phil wanted to move back home to their native South Carolina from Wisconsin. Family ties, old friends, and mild climate all called to them from Greenville, one of the larger cities in South Carolina and close to where both of them had gone to college. So they started with a destination in mind. They also had two years' lead time, so they decided to buy now and rent out their new home until they were ready to move. They chose a neighborhood of single family homes that provided yard maintenance and was located close to shopping and amenities. They also made a list of specific requirements that would see them into their later years, like a first floor bedroom and few steps. Rental income covered the mortgage for two years while they got their home in Wisconsin ready to sell. They cleared out the accumulated "stuff" from many unsorted corporate moves and from raising two children, and, two years later, they were in their dream retirement home.

Finding a Home that Meets your Needs

Finding the right home is a big deal, and it deserves your careful time and attention. Revisiting Myers-Briggs, we suggest that you approach the task something midway between the J personality's rush to decision and the P personality's endless gathering of information. If you have decided to stay in the area, friends and acquaintances can offer leads and suggestions based on their experiences. Read the real estate ads in the newspaper and on-line to get a sense of what's available in your price range and housing style. This will help you to narrow the search, and it's a good start.

Ultimately, though, you will want to work with a real estate professional to help with identifying and visiting possible future homes, figuring out the cost of any needed changes, working with the seller on repairs, and negotiating a price. Not every real estate agent is a Realtor, a member of the national Association of Realtors who has undergone a lot of training in the profession. Some Realtors or real estate agents work only for the seller, some only for the buyer, and some do double representation. A Realtor that you would like to have represent you as a seller, because she is aggressive about showing houses and getting the best price may not be the person you want working with you as a buyer. Talk to people about which Realtor would be the best one for you. If you are moving long distance but close to family and friends, they can help you determine what's available at your price range and find a Realtor who is a good fit for you.

You may want to work with a Realtor who is designated as a Senior Real Estate Specialist (SRES). You can locate one on the web site www.SeniorREalEstate.com. In any case, you will want to interview one or more prospective Realtors for both buying and selling, and you may want a different Realtor for each purpose, especially if you are moving out of the area.

One option we have not explored is building a home to meet your retirement needs. This is a complicated undertaking, but it is a good way to get exactly what you want. Expect it to take longer than buying an existing home, and be prepared for lots of decisions, changes in those decisions, and (if you have a partner) conflict, but it may be worth it in the end. Again, you will need recommendations on a contractor and location from people in the area.

Yet another option that some people may want to explore is shared living space with family members or others. This option is particularly useful for single adults in declining health who may want or need to have someone living very close by to help with any medical emergencies. Shared space may involve redesigning space in someone else's home or building something that meets the needs of everyone involved. In this case, your options are more limited, but you will still need to weigh the pros and cons against the other possibilities.

Choosing a Realtor or Real Estate Agent

If you are selling a home, and most readers will be, this is also the time to find an agent, preferably a Realtor, to help you sell your present home. If that person is going to be the same one who helps find your new home, you need to consider this person's skills and experience in selling other homes in the area. So be prepared to interview one or more Realtors before signing a contract.

Here are some questions you might want to ask:
1. What company and broker are you affiliated with?
2. How long have you been in real estate sales?
3. Do you work as a buyer's agent or a seller's agent or both?
4. How many listings do you currently have on the market?
5. What is the current Days On Market (DOM) for homes in my area?
6. Can you provide me with a list of homes that have sold in the last six months in my neighborhood/price range and how long they were on the market?

7. What is your marketing plan for the sale of my home?
8. Do you stage, or recommend staging, before listing the home? [Staging means reducing clutter, rearranging furniture, fresh flowers, and other ways of making the house look more attractive.]
9. Can you provide a list of references from previous sellers?
10. What commission do you charge?
11. How will my home be advertised in the MLS (multiple listing service), signage, on-line, open house, etc.?
12. What are the advantages of listing with you and your agency?
13. What things should be done to my house and property before listing?
14. What is the best time to sell my house in this market area?

De-Cluttering before Moving

Once you get into the house-hunting process, you may be more motivated to de-clutter your present house. NOW is always the best time to start the de-cluttering process, regardless of how soon you expect to be moving. Even if you have decided to stay put and retrofit your house for your future needs, the sooner you de-clutter, the sooner you will be able to begin enjoying the benefits of a clutter-free life. De-cluttering before moving helps ready your home for the market, and, if you need the proceeds of that sale to buy another home, remember that de-cluttering is essential to marketing your home.

If you are one of those people who has spent a very long time in your current home, has no mortgage, and is staying in the same area, there is an alternative strategy, which is move first, de-clutter later. While this is contrary to what we normally recommend, in some circumstances it may make sense to take what you need to the new home and then work through the stuff left behind. How long can you take? It depends on how urgently you need the cash from the sale of your new home.

If you are moving an aging parent, or if you need extra help yourself, you might want to use the services of a certified Senior Move Manager, a person trained and specializing in helping seniors relocate. There is a web site to help you find someone in your area. Check it out at www.NASMM.org.

Assignment: Choose an Option and Start Implementation

This chapter's first assignment is to make a decision. Remember that not deciding is a decision in itself. Not deciding may foreclose some options, as the available housing choices change and as you continue to grow older. So lay out the options: 1) stay put and retrofitting, 2) remain in your community but move to a home that fits your vision in the preceding chapter as closely as possible, or 3) relocate to a new community. Discuss these choices with your partner, if you have one, or your family and friends. Then write your decision in your journal with the reasons for that choice. Let it sit for a few days or weeks and revisit it to make sure it still feels right.

Once you are comfortable with the decision you've made, the next steps in your assignment are pretty obvious.

1. De-cluttering is an important first step, whether you are staying in your present home or moving. Start building a time line for de-cluttering that fits in with your moving plans.

2A. If you are staying put, it's time to seek professional help in planning changes to your present home and developing a financial plan for paying for those improvements. Take a page in your notebook or journal to list the kinds of changes you need and the kinds of professionals—plumbers, carpenters, painters—you will need to carry them out. Start getting recommendations and estimates.

2B. If you are looking for a new home, set a time frame for gathering information, on your own and from friends and others, and then find the right real estate professional to help you in your search. Talk to a mortgage banker about your financing issues and consider getting pre-approval for a mortgage. All of this will speed the process of actually buying your new home once you find the one you want.

PART V

Transitioning to a New Home

Nine

From Here to There

Find a way to remind yourself daily of the
value of the things you want and getting there
will seem effortless.—Author unknown

I f you have decided to age in place, you can stop here or
read on in case you change your mind later. For those of you
who have committed to moving, this chapter and the next are
the last two stages of your five-stage process strategy of downsizing and de-cluttering identified in Chapter 1.

If you don't own a home, the next step is obvious: find one.
But if you own a home, like most people who are at this stage
of life and reading this book, you have another decision to
make before you buy a house: should I move first and then sell,
or sell first and then move?

Sell and Move, or Move and Sell?

If you sell before you move, you are on safer ground financially, especially if you have a mortgage on your current home.
When you sell you are probably going to have to move fast in
terms of emptying your house, finding a new place to live, and
arranging financing if necessary. (Some sellers will agree to a

contract on the new home that is contingent on the sale of your home. And some buyers are willing to delay taking occupancy. (But don't count on either of those happening.) Sell first is often the preferred strategy for long distance moves and for homes that don't require a lot of work to make them market-ready. Realtors report that homes show better while occupied, which is another plus for this strategy.

A big downside for many homeowners, however, is that the house always has to be ready to show on fairly short notice. If you are living in your home while you sell it, it is especially important to de-clutter your house as much as possible before putting it on the market and continue to keep it orderly while waiting for a sale.

The second alternative is attractive to those who have been in their homes for a long time, because longtime occupancy usually means a home full of stuff and in need of upgrading and sprucing up before it is marketable. This alternative can be more challenging financially because you will have to come up with a down payment on the new place without having the equity in the old home to draw on, and you may be paying two mortgages until the old house sells. But it puts less time pressure on you, because you can empty the house more gradually and don't have to live in it while it is repaired, upgraded and painted to make it attractive to prospective buyers. It also may make it easier for you to let go if you already have a new home identified and under contract or construction.

The Financial Side: Transition Options

Finances are a major obstacle for many people in making the move from their current home to one more suited to this stage of life. If you have a mortgage on your home and you buy another one before your present home sells, you may be paying two mortgages for a while. Even if you don't have a mortgage, you will need a down payment on the new home and money to get your present home ready for the market.

AOL Real Estate (http://realestate.aol.com/blog/2013/05/06/) suggests that your strategy should depend on how competitive or slow the housing market is in the area(s) where you are buying and selling and the amount of home equity or other financial resources you bring to the table. If you can manage the finances, the choice to buy first gives you two sites to work with while you downsize and de-clutter. If you have substantial equity in your present home or have enough financial resources to buy before selling, that allows you to make an offer as soon as you find the right house. Don't wait to sell your house first. If you find your dream house but aren't ready to move, you can buy it and lease it while you sell your present home and prepare to move. This strategy was the one Fran and Phil chose in their move from Wisconsin to South Carolina.

If you need to move, however, and you don't have a lot of cash, your decision is more difficult. Buying before selling may mean tapping your 401(k) or other assets, although that's usually not such a good idea. A better choice, if it's possible, is to draw on your home equity line of credit in your present home to generate enough cash for closing costs and down payment.- If you don't have a home equity line of credit, be sure to get one before you go home shopping. But bear in mind that, if you follow this strategy, you may have three payments—your old mortgage (unless it is paid off), your home equity loan, and your new mortgage—at least for a short period. So run the financials before undertaking this approach.

You can also make a contingent offer, which means that your purchase will go through only if you succeed in selling your present home. Some sellers will be less receptive than others to a contingent offer, but it's worth a try, especially if the house you are buying has been on the market for a long time. In fact, it's a good idea to visit your mortgage lender and see how much they are willing to lend, a process called pre-qualifying. Here's a story that makes the point.

When Holley sold her house, she had two very interested buyers. She actually preferred one buyer over the other for sentimental reasons. She could tell he loved and appreciated the house, and it was perfect for his family's needs—fenced pet yard, lots of bedrooms, big kitchen, extremely convenient to work. This buyer was also willing to pay a little more. But the other buyer had pre-qualified for a mortgage and was ready to sign a binding contract, while the first buyer still had a home to sell elsewhere and wasn't sure he could afford two mortgages for more than a short time. He made an offer contingent on the sale of his present house. Needless to say, the house went to the buyer with the lower offer but the one that had a much better chance of resulting in a successful closing. Doing your financial homework before you go house-shopping puts you in a better situation if there is competition for the house you want to buy.

If you are in a slow sales market, you may want to list your home as soon as you can get it ready (see staging, next chapter) and postpone buying until you sell. If a buyer appears on the scene quickly, you may negotiate a delayed closing or rent back your home or, if all else fails, find temporary housing and storage space while you set out on an intensive search for your new home. You can also arrange with a bank for a bridge loan, but the interest rates on bridge loans are higher, and you will once again be paying off three loans during the transition. Bankers are familiar with this situation and may allow you to borrow at a higher than normal debt to income ratio, but, if the selling part drags on, you still face a lot of monthly loan costs.

In either case, you should try to time your sale when the market is strongest in your area, especially in smaller communities. Most markets are strongest in spring and early summer, especially for families with children who do not want to disrupt schooling.

Now that you have a sense of your options, gather your financial information—income, assets, and debts—and you are ready to have a conversation with a mortgage banking specialist.

Selling the Homestead: Letting Go

You may think you are ready to cut your ties to the old place, but sometimes the unconscious signals send a different message. Refusing to undertake changes that will make the house more attractive to prospective buyers is one signal ("they should love it just the way it is"). Setting the price unrealistically high is another. So, before you are ready to take the necessary steps to put your house on the market, you may need to work on letting go. Leaving your old home may be easier if you have not lived there a long time or if you have already located a new home. Letting go may require some help from your family and your support system; be sure to talk about the meaning and memories that this home holds for you, and find ways of preserving those memories with words or photos as you say goodbye.

Selling the Homestead: Making it Attractive

Repair and paint. These are typically the first order of business. It's easy to let certain maintenance tasks slide when you live in a house, but once you decide to sell, those broken door locks and missing screens need your attention. Paint, recarpeting (or at least carpet cleaning), and floor refinishing are obvious and not terribly expensive cosmetic improvements. Getting rid of pet odors is an absolute must. The yard needs to be spruced up and maintained during the sales period.

Major changes are another matter. Consult your real estate professional before buying new appliances, putting in new kitchen cabinets and granite countertops, or undertaking other major renovations. Expensive remodeling projects may make your home more appealing to some (not all) prospective buyers, but these efforts may price the house out of range for others. Also, many home buyers prefer to purchase at a lower price and do the renovations themselves.

If you are moving before selling, an empty house has certain advantages. Buyers are not distracted by clutter or existing furniture arrangements, but it may also make it more difficult for them to envision the house furnished, so you may want to leave some furniture behind until the house sells. Some people even rent furniture as part of "staging" their home to sell, because it is difficult to estimate the actual size of spaces without any reference points like a bed or a sofa. A dining room table with an attractive table setting and fresh flowers will make an impression on a prospective buyer. A vacant home will also require regular visits to deal with cobwebs or other problems. Cleanliness is essential, so you may want to invest your own time or hire a cleaning team to keep everything looking as appealing as possible.

If you are living there, the challenge is to hide the negatives. At least if the kids are grown and gone, that source of clutter and untidiness is no longer a challenge. Chances are you have plenty of clutter of your own, so getting rid of or at least hiding the clutter is a crucial part of staging.

First impressions are critical, and they are influenced by seemingly minor things, like light bulbs that need replacing or sticky cabinet doors. A tired sofa can affect the ambience of the whole room. The biggest issue, however, is clutter. Clutter is not just stacks of books and papers, but too much furniture for the room, dog beds and litter boxes and toys, too many knickknacks and other distractions. You may want to invite a friend or a professional with skill in decorating to look at your home and offer suggestions for making it more attractive to prospective buyers. There are web sites and staging professionals to help you in this process, or you can watch episodes of HGTV's program *The Stagers* for more ideas.

Other suggestions from staging professionals: repair any cracks and holes, paint with neutral colors, rearrange furniture to maximize space, organize closets and store out-of-season clothes elsewhere, remove family photos, and secure valuable items. Powerwash the exterior. Keep the entry and walkways swept and the lawn mowed, take care of the shrubs, plant seasonal flowers, hang fresh towels, and clean and organize the pantry, cabinets, and doors. You might even burn scented candles.

If prospective buyers have been watching Home and Garden TV, they may have high expectations of what the house should look like. In addition to the litany of open floor plan, stainless steel appliances, granite countertops, and updated bathrooms, some buyers also want a home that is turnkey-ready, with no work to be done on their part. Some buyers are willing to put in sweat equity in exchange for a lower price. Your Realtor can help you assess which is more likely in your neighborhood and price range.

Selling the Homestead: Realism and Prices

It's hard to be objective about the market value of something that carries so much emotional freight as a family home.

It's also hard to see a house that you have customized to your tastes, lifestyle, and family composition through the eyes of someone else whose tastes, lifestyle, and family may be quite different. The very things that make your house attractive to you may be a real turn-off for other people. So you are clearly not the best judge of what price to set. Remember, the right price is what the buyer will pay, not what you think it's worth. You might want to visit some open houses in your area to get an idea about prices for similar homes.

Your Realtor will help with "comps," or selling prices of similar homes in your area. But each house is unique, so pricing is discretionary, especially since you know that the price is open for negotiation. Set the price too high, and you may not attract any lookers. Set it too low, and you may sell fast but get less value out of your home than you could have. Once it's on the market, you will get a better indication of how close you are to its market value by whether it attracts few or many prospective buyers and what kinds of offers, if any, you receive.

Finding the New Place

Now that you have dealt with the old house, it's time to start looking for the new one, a task that, in reality, may be going on at the same time. Go back to your wish list and use it as a starting point. With help from friends, family, and/or a Realtor, settle on some potential neighborhoods or communities (gated or retirement) based on what you think is important—such as access to transportation, shopping and services, amenities, restrictions (zoning or covenant), lot sizes, and other relevant considerations.

Looking at houses is a volatile mix of reason and emotion. You may fall in love with a house without knowing why or reject another for seemingly trivial flaws just because it "doesn't feel right." But don't forget about your list of desired features; it is still important, so after looking at several houses, be sure to take a cooling-off period for a more rational evaluation of the pros and cons of each. In particular, identify the "turn offs" and ask yourself or your Realtor how costly they would be to fix. It's too easy to be turned off by a paint color or countertops that can be changed easily and inexpensively. Take another look at the vision you created, and ask yourself what each house has and doesn't have on that list. Buying a house is one of life's biggest and most expensive decisions. You don't want to make it in haste, but, if you've found THE house, you don't want to risk losing it either.

Making an offer and negotiating a deal is a complex process, one in which your Realtor should be helpful. Too low, and you may lose the house to someone willing to pay more; too high, and you will give money away unnecessarily. In addition to the price, there are other negotiable dimensions to the deal: help with closing costs, allowances toward a new roof or carpeting or bathroom remodeling, and, of course, repairs that may need to be made after a home inspection (a must do!!!).

From Here to There

The moving transition has just three parts: making the new home ready for occupancy, deciding what to bring with you, and deciding what to leave behind. Some things are easier to do in an empty house, like painting, recarpeting, tiling, or updating kitchens or bathrooms. If possible, you should do these things before you move in. Other changes can wait, because you can do them while you live there. A home inspection will identify things that need to be fixed. The cost of those repairs can be negotiated with the seller.

What do you bring with you? If you are really downsizing, you need to pick carefully. Some of your furniture may actually work better in your new space, while other pieces don't work at all. Measuring is important, but so is vision. Your vision won't be perfect, so expect to rethink some of those decisions after you have lived there for a while. Match your furnishings to the functions of each room, and find creative and satisfying ways of disposing of what you can no longer use (see Chapter 5 for suggestions).

Eyeballing is not a good approach for figuring out how your furniture will work in your new space. There are some great web resources for arranging furniture. Ikea and Copenhagen Furniture both offer free resources Autodesk Homestyler is a free tool that allows you to design a room in 3D or arrange furniture using a more traditional tool. You will need to measure the space and the furniture, but these tools will make the task of actually visioning the furniture in the space much easier.

If you have done your homework on de-cluttering, the move will be easier. If you haven't, you should tackle the task before you move into your new home. If there isn't enough time, you may have to put some of your things in storage. Don't automate that bill. Writing a check for it every month will remind you of the money you are wasting storing stuff you don't use. Identify the categories of clutter that you haven't finished when you move, and plan to address them as systematically and as promptly as you can. A lot of the joy of a new home can be diminished by too much stuff in too little space and too many boxes in need of emptying.

The move itself? That is probably easier than everything else you have had to do, because it doesn't involve as many decisions. Hire a reputable mover. Shop around for quotes, and ask friends and others for recommendations. If it's a local move, and if you have some time (especially if you are doing move first, sell later), you may want to handle some of the moving yourself. In particular, you may want to do some of your own packing, especially of items that are not fragile or valuable. You can get boxes on Freecycle, buy newsprint for wrapping cheaply at the local newspaper, and put clothes on hangers in the back of the car. Keep the pets, if you have them, out of the way during the move, and give them extra attention as they adapt to their new surroundings.

Assignment: Getting it Together and Staying Sane

This chapter outlined some specific tasks that you will need to address in the final stages of downsizing and de-cluttering. One is the financials. The other is the logistics of moving, including preparing your present home for sale and figuring out what goes with you to the new house. But it's also time for self-care, so that this new venture will be exciting and enjoyable, not just a lot of hard work.

Life is full of transitions, some big, some small. Transitions are stressful on individuals and on relation-ships. Be aware of the fact that buying and selling a home, acknowledging that you are entering a new and different stage of life, is a very big transition, one that deserves to be treated with respect, one that is fraught with emotion and conflict. How do you keep your balance during this transition? Everyone has to find their own answers, but here are a suggestions that might help:
1. Keep the lines of communications open.
2. Don't rush. You will be living with the consequences of these decisions for a very long time.
3. Take breaks. Go away for a day. Go to a spa for a mas-sage, manicure, and pedicure, or whatever turns you on.

4. Find a meaningful way to say goodbye to the old house. Take pictures. Transplant bulbs. Have a farewell party.
5. Celebrate the positive changes that are taking place. Celebrate your new space, which is a better match for who you are at this stage in your life.

PART VI

Settling In

Ten

Adapting to Your
New Space

*Be grateful for the home you have, knowing that
at this moment, all you have is all you need.—*
Sarah Ban Breathnach

The people in our focus groups who had been through downsizing were unanimous in having experienced a sense of freedom after reducing their "baggage." They felt relieved of possessions that needed to be cared for and that took up too much space, time, and attention. They also found they had a sense of adventure they had anticipated as they met new neighbors, explored new surroundings, and found new possibilities for living, working, playing, and enjoying relationships in their new surroundings. That's what you have to look forward to as you drive into the driveway and turn the key to your new front door.

Now you have arrived in your new space, unpacked most of the boxes, arranged the furniture, and are beginning to find the things that were put in strange places. You have met the neighbors, filled out the many change of address forms, and put the utility bills in your name. It's starting to feel like home.

What can you do to bring this long, complicated process to a happy ending?

Making It Yours

Part of feeling at home in the new space is making it yours. Put your mark on it—hang your pictures; splash your color choices on the walls; arrange your furniture and rearrange it; plant your favorite flowers in the yard. This step is the fun part, but it has its challenges. As you enter more fully into your new space you will discover things that you brought from the old space that just don't work, and other things that your new space will need. Perhaps those end tables from the old house are just too big for a smaller living room. The clusters of family pictures that were spread over a bigger space look crowded in a smaller one, and the herd needs to be culled. If unsorted clutter managed to follow you to your new home, it needs to be unpacked, sorted, and disposed of. Give yourself the best possible chance to enjoy your new surroundings by getting rid of the clutter before you get used to it. Also, give yourself at least six months of rearranging, discarding, and replacing to make the old you and some of the old stuff fit comfortably and attractively into your new space.

When Holley and Carl were first married, they rented a one-bedroom apartment. They cleaned it and polished it and furnished it with cast-off furniture from relatives. Then, with great pride, they welcomed Carl's parents to their new place. Pop immediately said, "It will look nice when you get it fixed up". Puzzled, Holley looked to her mother-in-law for a translation. "Oh, she said, he means curtains". Holley and Carl were graduate students on a limited budget, but they immediately put curtains at the top of the priority list.

Home means different things to different people. For some people, home means window treatments. They can represent completeness, boundaries, and self-expression. Figure out what means home to you. Invite friends over, one or two at a time, for tea or a glass of wine, and give them a tour of the new place. Ask for their ideas. They know you, know what you like and what makes you feel comfortable. Make them part of your new space.

Settling in: Getting to Maintenance

Once you are settled in, you may start to miss the novelty of arranging, decorating, and rediscovering your possessions. Don't let your home get stale. Move pictures around. Change the paint in the bathroom. Buy a new shower curtain. Rearrange the furniture. Five months into her new home, Holley regretted the decision to put her desk in the guest room; She couldn't access it when she had guests and she felt cut off from the main living space.- So she reconstituted the home office in the sun room just off the living room. An office is an important part of Holley's identity, and she realized the it needed to occupy a more prominent place in her new home.- A week of moving stuff around culminated in family help to move a futon and a desk, and both rooms became more attractive, more func- tional, and more what Holley wanted in a home.

You have been through the de-cluttering process. You've sorted, given away and sold things you never imagined you could part with. You've thrown things away that you'd held onto for years. And, much to your surprise, it feels good. But beware! Clutter has a nasty habit of sneaking back into your life. It will slide through the mail slot or follow you home from a sale at your favorite store. Especially if you've moved to a smaller space, it's important to take a stance against clutter. There are some good strategies for avoiding re-accumulation that you can adopt (or adapt to your personal style). Here is a list of possibilities:

- Need it? Rent it! Or borrow it. This strategy is particularly good for items you only need occasionally. Yard tools, extra tables and chairs, floor and carpet cleaning equipment, even a pickup truck are good candidates. So are boats and campers. Sharing with friends is also a good way to reduce the clutter of items that are only used occasionally.

- One comes, one goes. This strategy is especially good for books, magazines, and clothing. It's okay to buy new things, and it's much cheaper to subscribe to your favorite magazines than to buy them singly at the newsstand, but each new arrival means that something else needs to go in order to keep from re-accumulating. So when you come home from shopping, or the package or magazine arrives in the mail, you need to make a point of removing something equivalent. Put it in the trash or set it aside to be recycled or donated. It's especially satisfying to find an organization that would like your used magazines for their waiting room or their clients, and it makes it easier to let them go if you know they will be enjoyed by others.

- Paper clutter. Paper is a particularly big source of clutter, and it needs to be dealt with on a daily basis. If you are unsure of how to decide what to keep and how long to keep it, go back to Chapter 6 and review the information about managing paper. It might be a good idea to designate a particular day of the week for addressing any accumulated papers, but don't let that keep you from discarding or recycling newspapers and junk mail on a daily basis. Ideally, you only handle a piece of paper once!

- The pantry and/or kitchen and the bathroom are the primary places where consumables can accumulate. Spices and herbs have a finite lifetime. So do cosmetics and over the counter drugs. One good clutter manager declares an amnesty day every so often, for both her pantry and her bathroom, to dispose of expired food products, seasonings, medicines, and cosmetics. The refrigerator contains items that have the shortest lifetime, so de-clutter it weekly, but the pantry can probably get by with a monthly review and the bathrooms perhaps only every three to six months. If you haven't developed a strategy for managing perishable food, that's something you may want to introduce in your new home. This will both reduce food waste and de-clutter your refrigerator and pantry.

If you are a J on the Myers-Briggs scale, you probably respond to these ideas by making a schedule or designating a day to do the less frequent tasks like filing and "amnesty days" to dispose of items that have exceeded their shelf lives. Perhaps the last day of the month is amnesty day, or Monday is the day when you do recycling and donations. If you are a P, not so deeply into organization, but you do keep a calendar, perhaps you just need to write a reminder on the top of each month's calendar that you need to file papers and check the contents of the pantry and/or the bathroom cabinets that month. Eternal vigilance is not only the price of liberty, it's also the price of a clutter-free life!

Developing New Routines

Chances are you had routines for managing the household tasks at your old home. Whether you've moved or retrofitted, this is a new space with new rules. Sure, you still have a kitchen and at least one bathroom, but, especially if you've moved, there are probably fewer rooms, a different day for trash pickup, and fewer yard tasks. The Fly Lady book by Marla Cilley (see annotated bibliography) is especially helpful in showing you how to develop maintenance routines. Cilley's advice ensures that all parts of your home get regular but short bursts of attention and helps you create habits that keep clutter from rearing its ugly head!

Virtual Clutter: Dealing with Clutter in the Cloud

A lot of our paper clutter has been moved to our computers. Our correspondence is mostly email and Facebook, our photos are on our tablets or in albums on our desktop, and our physical space looks less cluttered as a result. But there are a couple of challenges here. One is getting rid of the clutter—the junk email, the many emails setting up meetings that have already taken place, the photos you don't want to keep. You may feel that your computer, unlike your home, has unlimited storage space. Certainly it has a lot, but too much stuff in your inbox or your photo files can make it difficult to find what you are looking for.

The second challenge is keeping some records in hard copy in case your computer crashes or you need to pass them on. Hard copy records are especially important for organizations where you play a leadership role. (An external hard drive backup is also a good idea.) So you may want to add to your regular schedule a time to de-clutter the inbox and the trash on your computer, which actually goes much faster than de-cluttering physical documents. You may also want to set up some folders on your computer to save things in categories, like travel, financial, etc. so that they are easier to find and easier to delete when the documents are no longer needed.

Assignment: Your Maintenance Plan

Only you can devise a clutter-resistant maintenance plan that works for you—one that suits your personality and that works with other people who may share your space. The specific suggestions offered in this chapter may or may not meet your needs, but they invite you to invent your own solutions, because the problem areas we identified are universal. Answering the questions listed below should help you formulate a custom maintenance plan.

1. What makes this new space feel like home?
2. How can we adapt the routes that helped to ensure order and comfort in our old home to our new space? What can we do about the danger of re-accumulation of books, magazines, and clothing?
3. How do we deal with foodstuffs, cosmetics, and medicines that have a finite lifetime?
4. What kinds of tools, equipment, and furnishings do we use infrequently and might want to rent as needed rather than find storage space for?
5. How do we stay on top of the flow of paper and virtual documents?

If you develop a plan or a strategy for each of those six categories, you will be on your way to a less cluttered life. The shared experience of our focus group participants and graduates of Fran's de-cluttering classes all testify that downsizing and de-cluttering are liberating, satisfying, and empowering. We hope that this book helps you to have that same joyful experience as well.

Smile—you are home! Enjoy!

Annotated Bibliography

aird, Lori (ed.), *Cut the Clutter and Stow the Stuff* (2002 Yankee Publishing, /Rodale Press. This edited volume focuses on cluttering styles of individuals and couples (Accumulators, Collectors, Concealers and Tossers) and describes a five step system of Quantify, Unload, Isolate, Contain and Keep it up (QUICK) for working through the decluttering process while getting the cooperation of other family members. Separate chapters for various areas of the house.

Carlomagno, Mary, *Secrets of Simplicity: learn to live better with less* (2008: Chronicle Books, San Francisco, CA). This workbook has headers of Release, Simplify, Treasure, Focus, Invest, Discover, and Thrive as Carlomagno leads you through lots of fill in the blank exercises to help you explore your relationship with stuff. She observes that we are overwhelmed by choice. We need to start with the way we live and work our way into the issue of possessions—what are our treasures? Cluttering is commonplace, hoarding has a pathological element to it. In decluttering, try emptying a room and make things earn their way back in.

Cilley, Marla, *Sink Reflections* (202: Bantam/Dell NY NY). The Fly Lady is a charming, encouraging guide to getting your house, your clutter, and your life under control one step at a time. Cilley leads you through the obstacles and how to change your habits with lots of hints, practical suggestions, pep talks, stories and letters. A very good chapter on controlling paper.

Dellaquila, Vickie, *Don't Toss My Memories in the Trash: A Step-by-Step Guide to Helping Seniors Downsize, Organize, and Move* (2007: Mountain Publishing). Dellaquila walks the reader through the choices and necessary steps to get from a home that no longer works for you to one that better meets your present and future needs, including paring down possessions. Lots of stories illustrate the choices and challenges. Pointers on using professionals at various stages of the process and how to find reputable services. Good checklists for moving "to-dos" and for choosing and placing the furniture to take to the new home.

Kingston, Karen, *Clearing Your Clutter with Feng Shui* (1999: Broadway Books, NY, NY). Although the emphasis is more on the clutter than the feng shui, this is an excellent guide to overcoming the mental, emotional, and spiritual obstacles to addressing the accumulation of possessions that gets in the way of having a comfortable and functional living space.

Kroeger, Otto and Janet M. Thussen, *Type Talk: The 16 Personality Types That Determine How We Live, Love and Work* (1989: Dell, NY, NY). A helpful guide to determining your personality type and how it explains how you engage the world, as well as how others engage it differently. Not a tool for judging, but for understanding yourself and others, that is helpful in many ways, including how we face life's challenges.

Lambert, Mary, *The ultimate guide to cleaning your clutter* (2010: Croc Books, NY, NY). This book will appeal to those attracted to New Age, aromatherapy, smudging, incense, and such eastern concepts as feng shui and chi that capture the Eastern spiritual dimensions of your relationship to your space and your possessions. Lambert sees clutter as a spiritual/psychological issue that interferes with the flow of chi (energy) She organizes the process room by room and project by project with quizzes, tips, routines, checklists, and pictures of what good rooms look like.

Leeds, Regina, *One Year to an Organized Life* (2008: MJF Books, NY, NY). This book is a gem for anyone looking for a structured plan to organize one's home and possessions, month by month, room by room, using dream boards and journals. Each chapter starts with questions and explores the roots of your feelings and where your habits come from. Takes up related topics like travel, entertainment, and holidays. Very good chapters on paper management and moving.

Melchior, Debra, *Organize Your Home!* (1992: Bob Adams Publishing, Holbrook, MA). If your big issue is managing the storage areas of your home rather than or in addition to decluttering, this book is for you. Twelve of the 28 chapters are devoted to clothing storage, with measurements and special topics like handbags and jewelry. Eight more chapters are devoted to kitchen and pantry. Lots of useful storage suggestions.

Morgenstern, Julie, *Organizing from the Inside Out 2nd ed.* (2004: Henry Holt). If you are looking for some good thoughts on the emotional/psychological obstacles to downsizing and decluttering, the challenge of working with a partner, and some very good ideas for how to proceed with the task, this book is an excellent resource.

Neergaard, Lauran (AP), "Home repairs help seniors maintain independence," *Anderson Independent Mail*, July 8, 2013, p. 9A.

Nemovitz, Bruce, *Moving in the Right Direction: The Senior's Guide to Moving and Downsizing*, Book Publishers Network, 2007, Bothell, WA. A short, useful guide to the process of relocating, either yourself or an aging relative, and some of the resources that can help in that process.

Palmer, Brooks, *Clutter Busting: Letting Go of What's Holding You Back* (2009, New World Library, Novato CA). This book deals with the emotional side of decluttering, answering the question of what is the reason you are attached to stuff in general or stuff in particular. It's a very psychological/emotional approach with lots of exercises and stories aimed at identifying the obstacles to decluttering.

Rohr, Richard, *Falling Upward: A Spirituality for the Two Halves of Life (2011: Jossey-Bass)*. If you want to explore the spiritual dimension of growing older, this book by a Franciscan priest speaks to people of all faith traditions about the tasks of letting go and leaving home.

Smalling, Donna, *The One Minute Organizer, Plain and Simple* (2004: Storey Publishing, North Adams, MA) and *Unclutter Your Home: 7 Simple Steps, 700 Tips and Ideas* (1999: Storey Publishing, North Adams, MA). These two little volumes are full of excellent specific suggestions. The earlier book also outlines a process for streamlining your home, but the major focus of both books is the specific ideas (like having a few rolls of all-occasion gift wrap instead of wrap that is for birthdays, weddings, Christmas...).

Tory, Moreen, *Going Forward: Downsizing, Moving and Settling In* (2012: Balboa Press/Hay House, Bloomington IN) This book is fairly light, but has some excellent specific suggestions on how to go through the process of downsizing in 6-12 months, particularly in planning your furniture, avoiding identity theft, and attaching a list of instructions to your will.

Ward, Lauri, *Downsizing Your House with Style: Living Well in a Smaller Space* (2007: Harper Collins, NY, NY). This book is about the appearance and arrangement of your new, smaller home from a decorating expert. Lots of pictures and ideas about how to decide what to take with you and how to use it most effectively.

Ware, Ciji, *Rightsizing your Life: Simplifying Your Surroundings While Keeping What Matters Most* (2007, Springboard Press, NY, NY). If you are an S (detail-oriented) and J (order and structure) personality type, this book will appeal to you. It is full of quizzes and good stories and excellent techniques for sorting through stuff. Also offers lots of resources for finding the people you need to help you through the process, including people who specialize in moving seniors or helping them adapt their house to present and future needs.

Winston, Stephanie, *Getting Organized* (1978: Warner Books, NY, NY). This classic book on organization is broader than organizing the home. It also addresses management of time and money, which involves the same principles or organization. Dated, but still a good read.

Notes

14324583R00085

Printed in Great Britain
by Amazon.co.uk, Ltd.,
Marston Gate.